RELATIVE CHRONOLOGIES

in

OLD WORLD ARCHEOLOGY

Edited by

ROBERT W. EHRICH

THE UNIVERSITY OF CHICAGO PRESS

930.02
E h 8 r
32554

July, 1955

Published in cooperation with the American Anthropological Association and the Archaeological Institute of America

THE UNIVERSITY OF CHICAGO PRESS, CHICAGO 37
Cambridge University Press, London, N.W. 1, England
The University of Toronto Press, Toronto 5, Canada

Foreword

The papers here presented were delivered at the Fifty-first Annual Meeting of the American Anthropological Association, in Philadelphia, on December 30, 1952. Together they constituted the structure of a symposium on "The Integration of Relative Chronologies in Old World Archeology," which was jointly sponsored by the American Anthropological Association and the Archaeological Institute of America. Fittingly enough, this co-sponsorship has been extended to the publication.

Since the dating systems of various areas are in a state of flux and since there are disagreements as to fixed dates, it was decided to eschew absolute chronology. The problem set was to progress through a series of more or less contiguous areas and to review the archeological sequences of each, concentrating on specific and documented materials which could be considered either as imports, exports, or of such close similarity to those of the others as to argue for a reasonable measure of contemporaneity. It was intended by this procedure to establish an interlocking network of chronological relationships, so that, as any particular stratum or period should be definitively and accurately dated, the corresponding periods or cross-dated complexes of neighboring areas would also fall into their proper places in terms of absolute chronology. The original prospectus of the symposium read, in part: "It is hoped that this program will help to co-ordinate the chronologies of Egypt and Mesopotamia, to link the sequences of outlying areas to those of the archeological heartland, and to focus attention on gaps in the record which should be filled by planned research." For such an approach it was obviously essential that the major emphasis should be placed on specific resemblances between relatively complex materials rather than on vague or more generalized similarities.

Since it was necessary to restrict each paper to one half-hour, limitations of time and space have precluded as detailed and lengthy analyses of certain points as one might wish. To some extent, therefore, and particularly with regard to the more controversial questions, much of the evidence was, of necessity, condensed, and much of what is here presented is summary in nature. There is, of course, a considerable degree of variation between the different areas in regard to cross-ties which will stand the acid tests of satisfactory documentation, limited duration in time, and a sufficient degree of complexity to justify assumptions of relationship and contemporaneity. Despite the vast areas covered, it is felt that the chronological structure as presented is such that others can and will build upon it, both elaborating in more detail the areas here discussed and extending it to include other regions which were not covered.

In varying degrees the contributors faced the twofold problem of reexamining the relative chronologies between the subregions of their own areas and of isolating demonstrable evidences of chronological relationship with neighboring ones. It must be stressed that although some questions of cultural dynamics were raised during the discussions, the object of the symposium was to integrate the relative chronological patterns as a working hypothesis, in order to provide a framework for future considerations of isolation, internal development, diffusion, and migration, together with their courses of direction. The primary purpose was thus limited to this one aspect, and there was no intention of trying to answer all the questions raised by the integration of the various chronologies. It is, of course, impossible to explain one's views on chronological problems in a complete vacuum and without recourse to some cultural interpretations and biases. However, all the papers hew closely to the line as originally set, and there is consequently a very real consistency of approach.

To a great extent the contributors regarded the general theme as a common problem rather than as a series of separate and isolated questions. Some of the papers with their accompanying tables were submitted early enough so that it was possible to reproduce and circulate them among the participants in advance of the meetings. There was also a considerable amount of correspondence among some of the members, although other papers were worked out completely independently. In a very real sense, then, the symposium represents a joint and co-operative effort. Inasmuch as the papers were written from the vantage point of different areas, it would be too much to hope that no discrepancies would appear. In view of some of the controversies now raging, it is really surprising that so large a measure of agreement was actually achieved.

As here arranged, the papers follow the same order in which they were presented at the symposium. It appeared most logical to start with Egypt, where the absolute chronology seems most trustworthy, and to work eastward across Palestine and Syria to Mesopotamia and the Iranian

Plateau. The afternoon session trended northward to the peripheries, beginning with southern Anatolia, traversing the Aegean to southeastern and central Europe, and finally to China. This sequence seemed to furnish the best system by which each paper could be progressively articulated with what had gone before.

With only one day available for the symposium, it was impossible to allow for more than nine papers, and thus some areas which it would have been highly desirable to treat were perforce omitted from the program. Of these, Anatolia proper, although a serious omission, is partly covered by reference in the papers on the surrounding areas. Eastern Europe, the western Mediterranean, and western Europe are frankly peripheral rather than links between the regions chosen. It is hoped that the co-ordinated chronological structure emerging from the symposium is such that the archeological sequences of these areas can eventually be tied to it.

Since the papers themselves are to some extent summaries and are, in turn, summarized by the accompanying tables, which interlock, it seems unnecessary to review them here.

Thanks to the kindness of the Wenner-Gren Foundation for Anthropological Research in the lending of a tape recorder, it was possible to obtain an almost complete transcript of the ensuing discussions. However, many of the points raised, although of interest, were not particularly relevant to the stated objective of the symposium, and therefore it seems advisable to refer briefly to a few of the more important items and not to reproduce the transcript in its entirety.

The major part of the general discussion revolved about the nature of the criteria used and the role played by cultural dynamics even in an effort limited to chronological interpretation. Some concern was voiced over the heavy emphasis on pottery, with the comment that a pottery style by itself does not constitute a culture. However, for the purpose of cross-dating, pottery does fill most of the requirements. It is short-lived, normally present in great quantity, usually well preserved once it has been broken, distinctive with regard to locality and period, and an inherently complex criterion, in that it is subject to infinite variation in technique, form, and style of decoration (Ehrich, 1950, pp. 476-77). While a pottery type admittedly does not constitute a culture, it is a valuable index criterion.

Some confusion seems to arise from differences in the application of the term "culture." Although in archeological or ethnological analysis it is used in Taylor's (1948) partitive sense to denote the patterning or total way of life of a specific group of people, it must be remembered that, so applied, the word is flexible and can be used with reference to almost any definable group and on almost any level of abstraction, provided that the level on which it is employed is adequately indicated.

During the last few years archeologists have become much more conscious of cultural dynamics, and they have shown a constantly increasing tendency to restrict the use of the term "culture" to broader aspects of consistency in the ways of life of larger and larger units. However, as long as it is proper to speak ethnologically of the culture of a village, as well as of the culture of a tribe or region, it seems perfectly in order to discuss archeologically the culture of a single site or of several village sites or cemeteries which are distributed throughout an area. This holds, despite similarities with other complexes in the general way of life, provided that such groups can be identified as entities, if only by common aesthetic traditions as reflected in the relative degree of identity in their ceramic wares. So used, of course, the ceramics themselves form trait complexes rather than cultures, but they do furnish criteria for isolating groups of people whose cultures can be discussed.

Since archeology deals with time depth as well as spatial distributions, it also seems admissible to use the term "culture" to delineate differences between periods as well as to express continuities of more general patterns in the way of life. Culture, then, is a sliding-scale term, and it is necessary only to make the order of magnitude explicit, to use it in a narrow sense without hesitation and without apology.

The cultural dynamics brought into focus by the challenge to the use of pottery, however, do pose serious questions as to identities such as those resulting from continuities of contact after migration; time lag from cultural borrowing; an even greater discrepancy caused by cultural conservatism in an isolated area where a tradition may continue relatively unchanged, while in the area of its origin it may undergo a series of relatively rapid sequential changes; and the synchronisms that can be established by proved imports and exports as opposed to those of more generalized similarity. Other criteria also pose the problem of individual, as well as cultural, longevity as opposed to the brief time span of a single pot.

It was precisely on these grounds that Dr. Albright questioned Dr. Weinberg's equation of Troy II and the VIth Dynasty of Egypt with the Royal

Tombs of Ur on the similarity of the jewelry. Jewelry, he pointed out, can remain in use for a long time after the death of the original owner, and the Royal Tombs, he feels, are definitely earlier.

Dr. Adams expressed concern at the assumptions of invasion from the Iranian Plateau to explain the early peopling of Mesopotamia, as opposed to the possibility of an original culture borrowing and a subsequent internal development such as he believes to have taken place in the Amouq during Phase E. Although the resolution of this problem is beyond the scope of the symposium, the fact that it was brought up does sharply delineate the necessity for establishing an unshakable structure of relative chronologies before such questions can be satisfactorily answered.

Another rather elementary point thrown into relief is that contiguous areas that are not too sharply set off by topographical features and that have easily traveled communication routes between them do have a tendency to furnish a greater quantity of direct imports than do those where the reverse is true. This holds particularly for such regions as the Middle Danube Basin, where the archeological exploitation of the intervening rugged territory of Macedonia is as yet insufficient to provide precise and indisputable links with the Aegean. China, of course, is even more remote, and the lacunae between the Far East and the West are both more numerous and greater in size, to say nothing of the gaps in the Far Eastern internal chronological systems. Thus the greater the distances to be spanned and the more difficult of passage the zones between, the greater must be the recourse to more general similarities in style and technology and the less detailed can be the demonstration of chronological equations of two or more areas until a step-by-step series of sites furnishes indisputable evidence of linkage. Thus the black and gray wares and the painted wares of Honan cited by Mr. Ward can indicate only rough relationships with the West until we have a much greater wealth of detailed stratigraphic material from Central Asia and from the various provinces of China itself.

By implication, Dr. Matson's comment, supported by Mr. Ward, that the gray wares of vast regions show a generic relationship based on a technical innovation in firing, includes in a general sense the more precise question suggested by Miss Goldman relative to the dating of Tepe Hissar by Dr. McCown (see Goldman, p. 75, and McCown, p. 61, below). Unfortunately, the striking similarities in form as well as in technique between the Grey Minyan wares of the Aegean Middle Bronze Age and Tepe Hissar found no place either in the discussion or in Dr. Weinberg's paper, which does not go beyond the end of the Early Bronze Age. These complex likenesses, as well as some Minoan shapes appearing at Tepe Hissar, have already been discussed in various publications, and the Tarsus spear point may furnish additional support for a lower dating than is generally accepted. Further concrete evidence from the areas between is badly needed.

It is to the answering of just such questions that a system of co-ordinated relative chronologies must serve as a preliminary step. With our present limited knowledge, many established sequences can be related to those of other areas at only a few solidly documented contact points, and others can be related only in a general way or by rule of thumb. As more data appear, however, the outlines here presented should become sharper, clearer, and more fully verified.

As the individual charged with the organization of the symposium and with the assembling of this publication, I wish to express my deep appreciation to the various contributors for their unfailing co-operation, and particularly to Dr. Goldman and Dr. Braidwood for their very generous use of their own material in advance of the final publications which they are now preparing.

Further thanks are due those who attended the symposium and those who took such a lively part in the discussion.

I would also like to express my gratitude both to Dr. Sol Tax, the editor of the American Anthropological Association, and to Dr. Richard Stillwell, of the Archaeological Institute of America, whose interest, assistance, and support have made this publication possible.

Robert W. Ehrich

Brooklyn College
July 1953

References

Ehrich, R. W. "Some Reflections on Archaeological Interpretation," American Anthropologist, LII, No. 4 (1950), 468-82.
Taylor, Walter W. 1948. A Study of Archaeology. ("Memoirs of the American Anthropological Association," No. 69; American Anthropologist, Vol. L, No. 3 [1948], Part 2.)

Editor's Note

In general, the stylistic practices of the University of Chicago Press have been followed for the sake of uniformity. Since usages with regard to spelling, punctuation, capitalization, bibliographical citation, and the like tend to differ among the areas represented by the papers, some violence to established local customs has been unavoidable. With reference to pottery terms, for example, there was little consistency from paper to paper as to the use of capitals or lower case. It was frequently difficult to tell whether a term was employed descriptively or categorically, and it therefore seemed wise to capitalize only those pottery designations which were used to identify cultural groups. On the other hand, some diversity remains, as in the rendering of proper names, and in so far as possible, such discrepancies are brought together in the Index. The editor accepts full responsibility.

Table of Contents

Page

The Chronology of Egypt and Its Correlation with That of Other Parts of the Near East in the Periods before the Late Bronze Age

Helene J. Kantor
Oriental Institute, University of Chicago

The Chronological Framework in Egypt

The chronology of Egypt is based upon indigenous historical traditions which were organized in the third century B.C. by the priest Manetho into a framework of thirty-one dynasties, stretching from the beginning of historical times through the Persian period. Except for phases of change and decline in the First and Second Intermediate periods and in the Late period, when rival dynasties ruled in a divided land, Egypt was, from the First Dynasty on, a unified country both politically and culturally. Thus, in contrast to western Asia, the difficult chronological problems of co-ordinating the dynastic sequences of contemporary states do not exist, except in the periods of decline. In addition to the general simplicity of the historical framework, the archeological material from Egypt has a peculiar character distinguishing it from that of most of the rest of the ancient Near East. In Egypt, with certain rare exceptions, we do not have stratified village or city sites, each with a sequence of levels which must be correlated, one with another, in order to give the internal archeological chronology of the country. The mass of archeological remains in Egypt, except for the great temples and a limited number of settlement sites, consists of cemeteries, aggregations of separate units, which must be arranged in sequence by the association of the individual grave groups with inscribed material and by typological study. Fortunately, sufficient evidence exists to make the general picture of cultural development clear, despite the uncertainties sometimes arising as to the exact position of specific graves or deposits.

Only in the predynastic period do we have in Egypt problems of internal chronology, the correlation of different sites; but even then they are minor in contrast to those of other countries. There were two distinct cultural traditions in the north and south, each comprising several stages (cf. Fig. 1). The sequence in the south, which Flinders Petrie originally established by typological means, has been verified by Caton-

Thompson's careful excavation of a small, stratified village at Hemamieh (Petrie, 1901, pp. 4-12; Brunton and Caton-Thompson, 1928, pp. 69-116). The complete northern sequence is not yet known; three distinct cultures occur in different, relatively small areas, without connecting links between them, except for the materials from El Omari, not yet published in detail but claimed to be a link between Merimde and Maadi (De Bono, 1945). The latest of the northern sites, Maadi, is clearly linked by types of pottery, stone vessels, and flints with the Gerzean period in the south, but its exact range in relation to that of Gerzean remains uncertain. The correlation of the earlier northern cultures with those of the south is not quite so unquestionable. However, there are certain features, such as the use of round huts, bowls supported by human feet modeled in clay, and carinated bowls, which point to an equation of Merimde with Amratian. No specific types of objects link the simple agricultural communities of Fayum A with the Tasian and Badarian cultures in the south; however, Fayum A is clearly earlier than the other northern cultures and is typologically very similar to the two earliest Upper Egyptian phases. Despite the tentativeness of some of these Upper and Lower Egyptian correlations, the general picture is clear. Prehistoric Egypt developed in a markedly homogeneous fashion, without the checkered variety of phases and the marked intrusions of alien cultures to be found in western Asia. Instead, there was only the gradual evolution of the northern and southern sequences. In the later part of the predynastic period north and south share more and more features in common, while the civilization of the First Dynasty was an immediate development of the Gerzean culture of Upper and Middle Egypt.

Both in prehistoric and in dynastic times, the clear-cut sequence of Egyptian periods provides a gauge helpful in establishing the chronology, both relative and absolute, of various other parts of the ancient Near East. Since this symposium is concerned with the problems of relative chronology, little need be said of the absolute chronology of Egypt, a subject ably summarized in various recent books (W. S. Smith, 1952, pp. 169-77; Drioton and Vandier, 1952, pp. 10-13, 156, 159, 627-32, and passim). Lists of kings and their regnal years, various types of contemporary documents, together with astronomical and calendrical data, provide the basis for Egyptian absolute chronology. The dates for the Twelfth Dynasty (Parker, 1950, pp. 63-69) and later periods are relatively certain, with only a small margin of error. The uncertain length of the First Intermediate period makes the dates for it and the preceding periods approximate only. The radiocarbon method of analyzing the age of organic materials promises eventually to provide approximate absolute dates for prehistoric periods. The few tests so far run on early Egyptian samples yielded the following dates (Libby, 1952, pp. 70-71):

Tomb of Hemaka, reign of Den, First Dynasty	$\left\{\begin{array}{l}3010 \text{ B.C. } \pm 240 \text{ years} \\ 2852 \text{ B.C. } \pm 260 \text{ years}\end{array}\right.$
El Omari; transitional Merimde-Maadi	3305 B.C. $\pm$ 230 years
Fayum A, earliest farming village in north	$\left\{\begin{array}{l}4103 \text{ B.C. } \pm 330 \text{ years} \\ 4440 \text{ B.C. } \pm 180 \text{ years}\end{array}\right.$

The Predynastic Period

It is possible to trace at various sites in Palestine and northern Iraq that crucial period in which "Neolithic" features—agriculture and the domestication of animals—developed, bringing the change from "food-gathering" to "food-producing." In Egypt materials of this period are unknown, being hidden presumably far below Nile silt. Whatever may have been the eventual sources of the "food-producing" economy in Egypt or the affinities of the most primitive agricultural communities in the country, by the time of the earliest village cultures which we know—Tasian, Badarian, and Amratian in the south, Fayum A and Merimde in the north—Egypt appears as an isolated corner of the Near East. Its local cultures flourished without any particular outside stimulation; even within the country contacts between north and south do not seem to have been very active. In general, it is likely that the affinities of these early Egyptian cultures will be found to lie with other African assemblages, such as those beginning to be known from the Sudan and Kharga oasis, though, as yet, it is perhaps premature to make a precise statement as to the relationships of these groups. In any case, although the early Egyptian villagers used some imported materials (for example, Red Sea shells, Sinai [?] turquoise and copper, even Syrian woods, such as pine, cedar, cypress, or juniper; cf. Brunton, 1928, pp. 41, 62 f.), there occur no objects of unmistakably foreign manufacture or type, with the exception of one isolated, and as yet cryptic, sherd painted with, Brunton considered, the representation of a high-hulled Mesopotamian type of ship (Brunton, 1937, pp. 83-84, Pl. 38, 4). Attempts to derive the painted pottery of Amratian, the white cross-lined ware, from that of various western Asiatic cultures seem quite unjustifiable to this writer (Baumgartel, 1947, pp. 54-71; Kantor, 1949, pp. 78-79).

The first clear evidence from Egypt of foreign connections occurs in Gerzean and marks it as a period of greatly widening horizons. One of the most prominent features in Gerzean, one distinguishing it from the parent Amratian culture, is a class of light-faced, ledge-handled jars. The first such jars to appear in Gerzean are squat and equipped with well-developed wavy or thumb-indented handles (Fig. 1, 50); they are comparable to Late Chalcolithic types in Palestine. In Egypt, such vessels and their handles have no prototypes, but in Palestine primitive ledge handles appear in the Middle Chalcolithic phase (Garstang, 1936, Pl. 32, 28, 29 A, B [Jericho VIII]; Fitzgerald, 1935, Pl. 2, 13, 14 [Beth Shan XVIII]); by the Late Chalcolithic period several developed forms of ledge handles—thumb-indented and wavy—were used on different types of vessels. Palestine must have been the source from which the ledge-handled jar reached Egypt, and it is interesting to note that the connection was sufficiently strong to stimulate the development of an entire class of Gerzean pottery in which the alien jar and handle shapes were gradually degraded.

In addition to the Gerzean sites of southern and middle Egypt, ledge-handled jars also occur in the north, at Maadi (Fig. 1, 36). At the moment there does not seem to be sufficient evidence to prove whether these Maadi examples are as early as those found in the south. This is an important problem, for it involves the question of the route by which Palestinian types of pottery entered Egypt. A priori, it seems likely that such vessels would have been introduced through the northern, Delta, part of the country.

Aside from the ledge-handled jars, the only other foreign feature to appear in the earlier part of the Gerzean period is a class of vessels with tilted spouts (Figs. 1, 51, 52; 2, M-O). Though made in an old, indigenous red polished ware, their spouts are completely un-Egyptian, and their prototypes must be sought in Mesopotamian vessels of the earlier part of the Protoliterate period (Fig. 2, P-R). Furthermore, it is possible that certain spouted vessels of the Late Chalcolithic in Palestine (Fig. 2, S, T) may also be influenced by the analogous Mesopotamian forms.

On the basis of the ledge-handled and spouted jars, the earlier part of Gerzean can be tentatively equated with the Late Chalcolithic period in Palestine and the Early Protoliterate (A-B) period in Mesopotamia. Now, though Gerzean is a fairly homogeneous culture, it is possible to distinguish earlier and later phases, that is, those graves belonging to Petrie's sequence dates 40-50 and those ranging from sequence date 50 to approximately 65. The later phase is marked by certain types of slender jars with rather debased wavy handles (Petrie, 1921, Pls. 28-29, Wavy 8-27); by the occurrence, in addition to the normal "decorated" ware, of vases with simplified patterns (ibid., Pl. 37, Decorated 78 A-F; Keimer, 1944, Pls. 1, 2); by elaborate ivory and stone carvings (Bénédite, 1916, 1918; Capart, 1904, pp. 224-25, Figs. 155-56; Pl. 1; Kantor, 1944); and by the appearance of a relatively large number of Palestinian and Mesopotamian features, which give clear synchronisms between the three areas. An important distinction between the foreign connections of Early and Late Gerzean should be noted. In the earlier period the two types of foreign pottery known were imitated by Egyptian potters, and examples are relatively frequent. In the later phase there are more foreign types of pottery, but they appear as individual examples, in most cases probably actual imports. Late Gerzean connections with foreign countries were apparently more frequent and perhaps more rapid than those of the preceding phase.

The Palestinian pottery types, all well known in Early Bronze I, occurring in Late Gerzean contexts are as follows: bowls with conoid projections (Fig. 1, 43), a form also found in Palestine in an exceptional instance in stone; a loop-handled cup and lug-handled pot with the red painting typical of southern Palestine (Fig. 1, 37, 40); and the latter shape without painting (Fig. 1, 41). Somewhat similar unpainted lugged pots and a loop-handled cup also occur at Maadi (Fig. 1, 33, 35), suggesting that that site was contemporary with Late Gerzean. In addition, variations of the spouted type already cited continue in Egypt (Figs. 1, 44; 2, I), Palestine (Fig. 2, L), and Mesopotamia (Fig. 2, J, K) in Late Gerzean, Early Bronze I, and Late Protoliterate (C-D) contexts. The equation of Late Gerzean (ca, S.D. 50-65) and Early Bronze I in Palestine is clear.

Mesopotamian connections are illustrated by a number of features of Late Gerzean. Most important for establishing a synchronism are the four cylinder seals of Jemdet Nasr style (imports and imitations), two of which occur in well-documented Late Gerzean graves (Fig. 1, 49). Since in Mesopotamia such seals belong to the later part of the Protoliterate period, the correlation of Late Gerzean with Protoliterate C-D can be set up with confidence. In addition to the seals, we also have from Egypt three examples of jars with four triangular lugs, a type known throughout the Protoliterate period (Figs. 1, 42, 45; 2, A, E, F; Delougaz, 1951, pp. 39, 134). However, the pot from Mostagedda (Fig. 2, A) is almost identical with Late Protoliterate vessels from Jemdet Nasr (Fig. 2, B, C; cf. also

D). The Badari vase is matched in shape, incised band, and plastic knobs
by a pot from Telloh (Fig. 2, G; cf. also H). The Badari and the Mostagedda vessels are both from undatable contexts; but, fortunately, we now
have a third pot with four lugs, from Matmar, which is dated to S.D. 58
(Fig. 2, F). It indicates that the other two specimens also date to Late
Gerzean, and all three are links with the Late Protoliterate period. It
should be mentioned that certain other Egyptian vessels, crudely made
bowls of the "Rough" and "Late" classes with angular rims (Petrie, 1921,
Pls. 38, 26 B, C; 45, 7 D, E, G), have been connected with Mesopotamia—
in fact, even claimed as examples of the famous beveled-rim bowls characteristic of the Protoliterate period (Baumgartel, 1947, p. 93; Burton-
Brown, 1948, pp. 247 and n. 12, 263, 266; Burton-Brown, 1946, pp. 36-37,
also quoted Protodynastic and Old Kingdom bread pots as pertinent examples). This correlation must be emphatically denied. Any seeming similarity between the two classes of bowls is purely illusory, a misappre-
hension presumably caused by comparison of simplified line drawings. In
their thickness, broad beveled rims, and specific formation (Delougaz,
1952, pp. 39, 127-28; Pls. 21, 168, C.002.210) the Mesopotamian bowls are
completely unlike any bowls known from Egypt. So far, Hama remains the
farthermost western site yielding beveled-rim bowls (Delougaz, 1952, Pl.
168, C.002.210).

The remaining Mesopotamian features of Late Gerzean are of a more
complicated nature (Frankfort, 1951, Appendix). They are the Mesopotamian high-hulled ships (Fig. 1, 39) and motifs—the "Gilgamesh" group,
in one case with the hero dressed in Mesopotamian costume (Fig. 1, 48);
the serpent-necked panthers (Fig. 1, 46); the entwined snakes (Fig. 1, 47)
—represented in Late Gerzean paintings and carvings (Hierakonpolis painting; "Decorated" vase of the simplified style in the British Museum [Fig.
1, 39]; Gebel el-Arak and Gebel Tarif knife handles; Small Hierakonpolis
and Four Jackal palettes). Some of these motifs, particularly the hero of
the Gebel el-Arak knife handle (Fig. 1, 48) and the entwined snakes of the
Gebel Tarif handle (Fig. 1, 47), are most closely paralleled on Early Protoliterate works. It is not surprising that such motifs should appear in
Egypt somewhat later than in Mesopotamia. They were carried abroad in
the Late Protoliterate phase, which was a period of tremendous expansion
of Mesopotamian civilization.

The inferences for comparative chronology of the evidence just cited
are clear; Late Gerzean in Egypt must be approximated with Early Bronze

I in Palestine and with the Late Protoliterate period (the former Jemdet
Nasr period) in Mesopotamia. It is not quite so easy to interpret this evidence in terms of cultural history. It appears that, though Egypt had now
emerged from its earlier isolation, the foreign influences, as far as can
be judged on the basis of the available archeological material, still formed
only fairly incidental or catalytic elements supplementary to the main
stream of indigenous development. Important unsolved problems are the
circumstances under which these features reached Egypt and the routes
by which they came. The old theory of a new invading race, for which the
obverse of the Gebel el-Arak handle has been cited, can hardly be upheld;
it is more likely that small groups of traders and travelers entered the
country, bringing about an exchange of objects and materials. For the
routes by which foreign influences reached Egypt, the evidence is only
slowly accumulating. It has been only natural to assume that a likely way
for Asiatic features to enter Egypt was through the eastern Delta, and we
now have a concentration of Palestinian features at Maadi, which could
serve as support for such a view. It should be noted, however, that, so
far, no Mesopotamian traits have been recorded from Lower or Middle
Egypt. Though this could easily be a mere accident of preservation and
discovery, it is equally possible that Palestinian and Mesopotamian char-
acters came in by different routes. In view of the representations of the
Mesopotamian ship type in Upper Egypt, not only on the works already
cited but also on desert rocks (Winkler, 1938, pp. 26-27, 35-39, Pls. 37 ff.),
it is likely that Mesopotamian influence was borne by sea to Upper Egypt.
A recent survey of the eastern desert between Koptos and Kosseir on the
Red Sea has proved that this route through the Wadi Hammamat, which in
historical times was an important line of communication linking sea-borne
traffic with the Nile Valley, was already marked out in the predynastic period by graves and village debris (De Bono, 1951).

The Protodynastic Period and the Old Kingdom (Early Bronze Period)

Egypt's connections with the Mediterranean littoral and Mesopotamia,
which began in Early Gerzean and were intensified in Late Gerzean, enter
a third stage in the First Dynasty. Mesopotamian influences seem to taper
off. The few persisting examples of motifs introduced earlier are relatively inconspicuous, with the exception of the serpent-necked panthers on the
Narmer palette. The foreign cylinder seal has been fully acclimatized by
the substitution of Egyptian motifs for the foreign ones. As far as pottery
is concerned, certain "cut-ware" braziers or stands known in Mesopotamia

in the Protoliterate and Early Dynastic periods may be connected with Egyptian braziers of the First Dynasty (Delougaz, 1952, p. 134; Frankfort, 1924, Fig. 13; Petrie, 1921, Pl. 51, Late 84b, 85). There is only one new trait of Mesopotamian origin, the elaborately recessed brick tombs in Memphite cemeteries (Fig. 1, 31) and at Naqada, the earliest monumental constructions in Egypt. As Frankfort has shown (1951, Appendix), they resemble Protoliterate temples closely in their exterior plan and in the construction of the niches. In Mesopotamia the prototypes of such niched buildings can be traced early in the Ubaid period, far back in prehistoric times. In Egypt, niched tombs appear suddenly without any antecedents— the primitive bricks from Merimde and Maadi can hardly be construed as such—at the beginning of the First Dynasty, immediately after the well-documented Mesopotamian connections of the Late Gerzean period. Unfortunately, there is no evidence as to the means of transmission, though it is likely that the thoroughgoing adoption of a complicated style of architecture entailed the traveling of skilled craftsmen. Apparently, the connections with Mesopotamia were not ordinary commercial ones; we find in the First Dynasty no Mesopotamian small objects or imported pottery vessels.

In strong contrast to Egypt's relations with Mesopotamia, its cultural peer, were those with Palestine and Syria. Here there was a more prosaic situation, the exploitation of the resources of a peripheral area by a strong central power. Instead of the sporadic Palestinian pots found in Gerzean, in the First Dynasty fairly large numbers of Syro-Palestinian vessels occur in kings' and noblemen's tombs and also in humbler, "middle-class" burials. Imported oils or perfumes were probably contained in the standard group of forms—loop-handled jars, smooth or combed (Fig. 1, 24, 25), flasks and pitchers (Fig. 1, 26, 27), some of which have narrow stump bases (Fig. 1, 29, 30). In addition to the plain gray, brown, and red-slipped wares, there is an outstanding group of painted pottery having chiefly geometric patterns in red or brown paint on a cream slip. Pitchers are the most frequent shapes (Fig. 3, A, B, E-H), but a jar with four loop handles also occurs (Fig. 3, C). So far, most examples of this ware have been found in Egypt; but as long ago as 1924 Frankfort pointed out that it was a Syrian product (Frankfort, 1924, pp. 108-10). In Palestine it also looks like an import, a rare one: a pitcher (Fig. 3, D) and biconical pot were found in a tomb at Kinnereth near Beth Yerah (Fig. 3, D; Maisler, 1942, Pl. 1, 44, 45). Actually, such pottery is relatively rare in the Amuq also (Fig. 3, I, J); it must have been produced in some part of Syria, presumably in the south, not as yet known from excavations. In addition to the imported pottery, the widespread use of Syrian timber in the First Dynasty and the finds of Egyptian objects at Byblos in southern Syria provide further evidence for the establishment of commercial relations with Syria.

The synchronization of the First Dynasty with other areas is rather precise, even though the niched brick architecture, since it is a prominent feature in both Protoliterate and later times, does not provide a chronological link with Mesopotamia. Early Bronze I in Palestine overlapped with the very beginning of the First Dynasty, as shown by a painted flask from Abusir el Meleq (Fig. 1, 32), a successor to the southern Palestinian painted vases found in Late Gerzean graves. The mass of foreign pottery from the First Dynasty tombs, however, is paralleled by Early Bronze II material from Palestine and southern Syria. In the Amuq, combed jars and Syrian bottles, both the plain ones and the painted variety whose exact source is still uncertain, occur in the later part of Phase G and in Phase H (cf. R. J. Braidwood, p. 38, below).

At present, there are no examples of foreign pottery from Second or Third Dynasty contexts. Either the demand for Syro-Palestinian products which had been so strong during the First Dynasty had now come to an end, or, the far more likely explanation, the pertinent material is not yet available from Egypt. Our knowledge of the archeology of the Second Dynasty is particularly limited; even for the Third Dynasty we do not have such an extensive series of pottery types as in the First Dynasty. Despite the present absence of imported objects in the later part of the Protodynastic period, it is evident that Egypt was still in contact with the Syro-Palestinian area. The timber indispensable for any ambitious building project was available; at Byblos was found a stone vessel fragment with the name of Khasekhemui of the Second Dynasty (Dunand, 1939, pp. 26-27, Pl. 39, 1115), and there are Egyptian stone vessels from Ai (cf. W. F. Albright, p. 30, below). However, on the basis of the material presently available from Egypt, no definite synchronization of the Second and Third Dynasties with Palestine and Syria is possible by direct means; but these dynasties may be presumed contemporary with Early Bronze II, since the Old Kingdom must be correlated with the Early Bronze III period in Palestine.

The Egyptian evidence for synchronizing the Fourth, Fifth, and Sixth Dynasties with Early Bronze III in Palestine comes chiefly from the royal necropoleis of Giza and Saqqara, where tombs of these periods contain large, loop-handled jars, frequently combed (Fig. 1, 19), and one-handled pitchers (Fig. 1, 20, 21), the EB III continuations of types already known from the EB II pottery imported during the First Dynasty. Occasionally, as at Matmar, such a foreign vessel will occur in a small private grave. One vessel from Giza (Fig. 1, 22) even provides a connection with Cilicia (cf. H. Goldman, p. 73, below).

In addition to the actual pottery and to the record of a timber-collecting expedition of Snefru on the Palermo stone, reliefs from the funerary temple of Sahure at Abusir illustrate Egypt's foreign connections. Ships returning from an Asiatic journey, as well as part of the Syrian produce brought back—bears and one-handled flasks (Fig. 1, 23)—are shown. It is likely that commerce with the east was exclusively carried on by state expeditions at this time. In view of these foreign connections in the Old Kingdom, it is rather disappointing that the types of foreign objects known from Egypt itself are relatively limited.

The Old Kingdom was followed by a period of change and decline, the First Intermediate period, when the central government broke down into small rival kingdoms. The Admonition of Ipuwer suggests that the turmoil throughout the land was heightened by incursions of Asiatics; but the attempts made to trace their presence by archeological means have not been successful. There are no unmistakably foreign types of objects known from the graves of the First Intermediate period. It is true that this period is characterized by a class of stamp seals which may find parallels elsewhere, particularly in Crete (cf. Goldman, p. 73, and Weinberg, p. 90, below). However, this is a difficult question which we will not explore here.

The Twelfth Dynasty and the Second Intermediate Period (Middle Bronze Period)

Not until the height of the Middle Kingdom, during the Twelfth Dynasty, are clear evidences for foreign connections again found within the borders of Egypt. These foreign objects from Egypt can be fully evaluated only when taken together with the Egyptian small objects and inscribed statues found in Crete, Palestine, Syria, and even as far north as Anatolia (Porter, Moss, and Burney, 1951, pp. 381, 386-87, 392-93; Pendlebury, 1930, p. 115). Clearly, the intensity of connections now was far greater than in the Early Bronze period. It has even been suggested that Egypt may have established some sort of organized rule in Palestine and Syria, but this is by no means certain.

Amenemhet II deposited in the Montu Temple at Ṭod four bronze chests containing a treasure of cylinder seals, small carvings, and silver vessels, which are the first actual examples of those Minoan metal vessels hitherto known only from pottery imitations of the Middle Minoan IIA and later periods (cf. De la Roque, 1950, for that part of the treasure in the Cairo Museum). Characteristic forms for the delicate Kamares ware of Middle Minoan IIA are bowls and cups similar in shape to the Ṭod silver vessels and with painted designs patterned after the plain or torsional fluting of metallic models (Evans, 1921, p. 241, Fig. 181; Pl. 2, a; Sup. Pl. 3, b; Evans, 1935, p. 132, Fig. 100; compare De la Roque, 1950, Pls. 12, 70580; 13, 70583; 16, 70619; 17, 70623, 70624, 70627, 70629). Also found at Tod was a cup with "Vaphio handle," for which the earliest-known Minoan parallel happens to be a Middle Minoan IIIA imitation in pottery of a metal prototype (Evans, 1921, Fig. 183, b, 1, opp. p. 242), so that we must rely upon the Ṭod specimen itself as proof that this typical Minoan handle type was already known in Middle Minoan II. In any case, the Ṭod find indicates that the first phase of Middle Minoan II existed at least as early as the reign of Amenemhet II in Egypt. The Minoan vessels of the deposit may not have reached Egypt directly from Crete but by way of western Asia, for the chests also contained some cylinder seals of the time of the Third Dynasty of Ur. If we assume that these Ur III seals represent the current glyptic of Mesopotamia and are not survivals from a somewhat earlier period—cylinder seals are notorious for their frequent persistence and must be used for chronology with due caution—we gain the approximate synchronism of the earlier Twelfth Dynasty with the Third Dynasty of Ur, on the one hand, and with Middle Minoan IIA, on the other.

The new Minoan-Egyptian correlation provided by the Ṭod treasure supplements the information given by the three much-discussed occurrences of Middle Minoan II pottery in Egypt (Pendlebury, 1939, pp. 144-45; S. Smith, 1945, pp. 1-3; Matz, 1950, pp. 173-74), pushing back the existence of Middle Minoan IIA to at least a period contemporary with Amenemhet II. Previously, the earliest-known date for the importation of Minoan objects was the reign of Amenemhet II's son, Sesostris II. Middle Minoan IIA sherds from Harageh were found in isolated shallow dumps of town debris, not associated with any houses (Fig. 1, 17). Aside from certain coarse Twelfth Dynasty pottery types, the only datable object in the dumps was a stone with the name of Sesostris II, whose pyramid and pyramid town lie in the neighborhood. The second Egyptian site with Minoan pottery is in the south, at Abydos, an indication of the wide distribution of Minoan ceramics in Egypt; the bridge-spouted jar in question, of a transitional (Middle Minoan IIA-B type (Fig. 1, 18), unfortunately comes from a shaft in a disturbed tomb, other shafts of which contained cylinder seals with the names of Sesostris III and Amenemhet III, dates which cannot be assigned with certainty to the Minoan vessel.

The third find of Minoan pottery, in this case belonging to the Middle Minoan IIB phase (Fig. 1, 12, 13), was made in rubbish heaps outside the pyramid city of Sesostris II at Kahun, a settlement occupied not only during the reign of that king but also in the Second Intermediate period. These rubbish heaps contained Middle Cypriote (White Painted V) and Syrian sherds of types that could hardly be earlier than the Second Intermediate period, thus contradicting Petrie's belief that these heaps must have belonged around the reign of Sesostris II, at a time when the city was still fully occupied so that debris had to be dumped outside the settlement instead of being thrown into empty houses. Thus the exact date of the Middle Minoan IIB sherds is uncertain and consequently also the range of Middle Minoan IIB, in so far as it is to be derived from the Egyptian evidence. Despite this imprecision, the general synchronization of Middle Minoan IIA with the earlier part of the Twelfth Dynasty and of Middle Minoan IIB with the end of the same dynasty is clear.

In addition to the foreign sherds already mentioned, the Kahun heaps and the village proper contained examples of a famous type of Syro-Palestinian pottery, the black, incised, and white-filled "Tell el Yahudiyah" ware, which usually occurs in the form of juglets. In Egypt this ware was commonest during the Second Intermediate period, and there has been considerable uncertainty as to when it first appeared, both there (Engberg, 1939, pp. 26-28; Säve-Söderbergh, 1941, pp. 124-26) and also in the East, where there are only a few possible examples in Middle Bronze IIA (Loud, 1948, Pl. 11, 1 [Megiddo XIV]; Chehab, 1939 [Sin el Fil]). With these latter finds could be correlated the equally sporadic Tell el Yahudiyah juglets attributed to the Twelfth Dynasty (Fig. 1, 11; Randall-MacIver and Woolley, 1911, Pl. 92, 10869, 10875) to form evidence from Egypt for the equation of Middle Bronze IIA with the Twelfth Dynasty. However, in view of the questionable dating of the presumed early Tell el Yahudiyah juglets, they provide but tenuous testimony and may be, for the moment at least, disregarded, particularly since the synchronism of the Twelfth Dynasty with Middle Bronze IIA is quite certain on the basis of discoveries made outside Egypt (cf. Albright, pp. 31-32, below).

It would perhaps be misleading to say that in the Second Intermediate period Egypt's connections with Syria and Palestine gained a new intensity. There had already been intimate connection in the Twelfth Dynasty, but then the relationship was that of a dominating power, traces of whose influence are found in client areas (statues of Egyptian officials and princesses, Egyptian gifts in royal tombs at Byblos, and the like), while in Egypt itself there are only instances of imported luxury objects (silver vessels; thin Kamares ware). Now, in the Second Intermediate period, the case is altered. In this period of political instability and foreign domination, we have the beginnings of widespread commerce linking Egypt, Palestine, Syria, and Cyprus. Thus in many Egyptian and Nubian sites there are examples of Middle Bronze IIB Syro-Palestinian pottery—Tell el Yahudiyah juglets (Fig. 1, 6, 7), plain red polished juglets (Fig. 1, 5), painted juglets (Fig. 1, 3, 4) and flasks (Fig. 1, 2), and vessels closely related to Cypriote White Painted V ware (Figs. 1, 1; 5, A). In addition to these normally found foreign types, there occur in Egypt a few vessels painted with designs characteristic of the Tell el Ajjul ware in Asia (Säve-Söderbergh, 1951, p. 58; Heurtley, 1939), though not executed in bichrome paint (Fig. 5, B-E). In Egypt such vessels can be assigned to the latest part of the Second Intermediate period; one of them (Figure 5, C) was described by Petrie as a "Syrian flask of the XVIIIth dynasty" (Petrie, 1914, p. 12). Since the Tell el Ajjul ware in Palestine, Syria, and Cyprus is typical of Late Bronze I, we have in the pots of Figure 5, B-E, evidence showing that the beginning of Late Bronze I in western Asia overlapped with the end of the Second Intermediate period in Egypt, a synchronism not indicated in Figure 1 for lack of space. All the vessels cited, both the actual imports and those showing the influence of foreign prototypes, illustrate the beginning of that intense international trade and communication which was typical of the late Bronze period and was not checked until the catastrophic incursions of Sea Peoples at the end of the Nineteenth Dynasty.

What is perhaps the most remarkable of the foreign vessels assignable to the Second Intermediate period is a jar from the excavations of the Metropolitan Museum of Art at Lisht, not yet published in detail. A tomb shaft (879) near the northern, Amenemhet I, pyramid, apparently made during the Twelfth Dynasty and containing some Twelfth Dynasty types of material, seems to have been either reused in the Second Intermediate period or contaminated by pottery from the Second Intermediate period vil-

lage that existed in the area. The shaft contained, in addition to Tell el
Yahudiyah juglet fragments, a vase unique in Egypt but belonging to a typical Palestinian and Syrian type known at the end of the Middle Bronze IIA
period, but common in Middle Bronze IIB (Fig. 4, D-F). This vase is not
merely a normal import from Palestine, however, but is outstanding for
its decoration—decoration utterly unparalleled in both Egypt and Palestine (Fig. 4, A, B). The designs are executed in a red wash, with borders
and interior details incised and filled with white pigment. Though the un-
gainly geese seem unparalleled, the dolphins are somewhat clumsy imitations of Middle Minoan IIIB dolphins, motifs borrowed from wall paintings
by the Minoan pot painters. In technique the Lisht dolphins have affinities
both with their white-outlined Minoan prototypes and with the incised,
white-filled decoration of Tell el Yahudiyah juglets. The synchronism between the Second Intermediate period in Egypt, Middle Minoan III in Crete,
and Middle Bronze IIB in Palestine is, of course, already well established
by other finds in Egypt and elsewhere, but the dolphins of the Lisht jar are
the first Middle Minoan III feature to be discovered in Egypt. Thus they
form a most welcome counterbalance to the evidence for Egyptian, and also Syrian, influence on the development of the representational art of Middle Minoan III. The Lisht find provides what might hardly have been expected, the epitomization on a single vase of the intimacy of connections
between Egypt, Syria-Palestine, and Crete in the final phase of the Middle
Bronze period.

Satisfactory as are the archeological correlations between the western
countries of the Near East in the Middle Bronze period, a sufficient number
of direct links between these coastal areas and Mesopotamia is still lacking. So far, we have only the Ur III seals from Ṭod as direct connections,
still somewhat tentative, between Egypt and Mesopotamia in the earlier
part of the Middle Bronze period. We have nothing comparable for Middle
Bronze IIB, but there is a pertinent discovery from southern Syria. Tomb
66 at Kafer Garra contained a typical assortment of Middle Bronze IIB pottery, including types commonly exported to Egypt, a number of scarabs of
Second Intermediate period types, and a cylinder seal of the First Syrian
group (Guiges, 1938, pp. 40-49). Now such Syrian cylinder seals are de-
pendent upon the glyptic style of the First Dynasty of Babylon (Frankfort,
1939, pp. 252 ff.), so that the Kafar Garra cylinder seal does serve as a
link, albeit an imprecise one, between the Second Intermediate period, Middle Bronze IIB, and the Old Babylonian period. Its testimony is strengthened

when it is recalled that in the murals of the Mari palace, contemporary with Hammurabi, there appear sphinxes and peculiarly artificial trees, both motifs explainable only as a result of contacts with that hybrid Canaanite art which developed in Middle Bronze IIB. Thus such evidence for the exchange of cultural and artistic influences can, to a considerable extent, substitute for the still missing direct links, which would be provided by the discovery of imported Mesopotamian objects along the Mediterranean littoral or in Egypt.

With the end of the Middle Bronze period, we have reached a time when the archeological evidence for comparative chronology is, except for the Aegean area, but a supplement for the detailed synchronisms given by written historical sources, a situation in strong contrast to the earlier periods, those we have surveyed here, where archeological evidences are the primary sources for relative chronology.

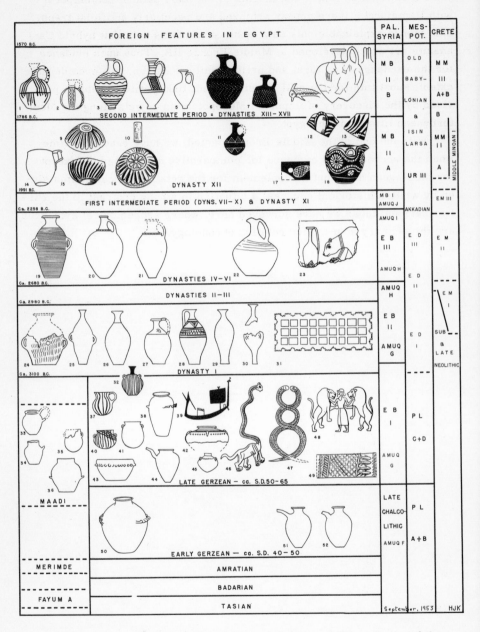

Fig. 1.—The Relative Chronology of Egypt and Other Parts of the Near East through the Middle Bronze Period.

EGYPT (A,E,F,I,M-O)　　MESOPOTAMIA (B-D,G,H,J,K,P-R)　　PALESTINE (L,S,T)

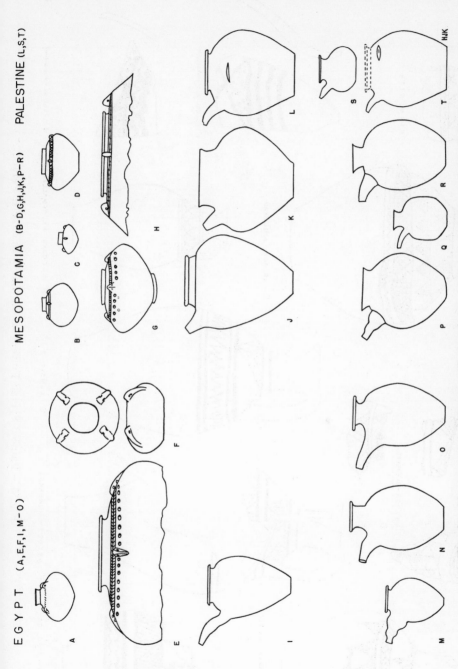

Fig. 2.—Mesopotamian Pottery Types in Prehistoric Egypt and Palestine

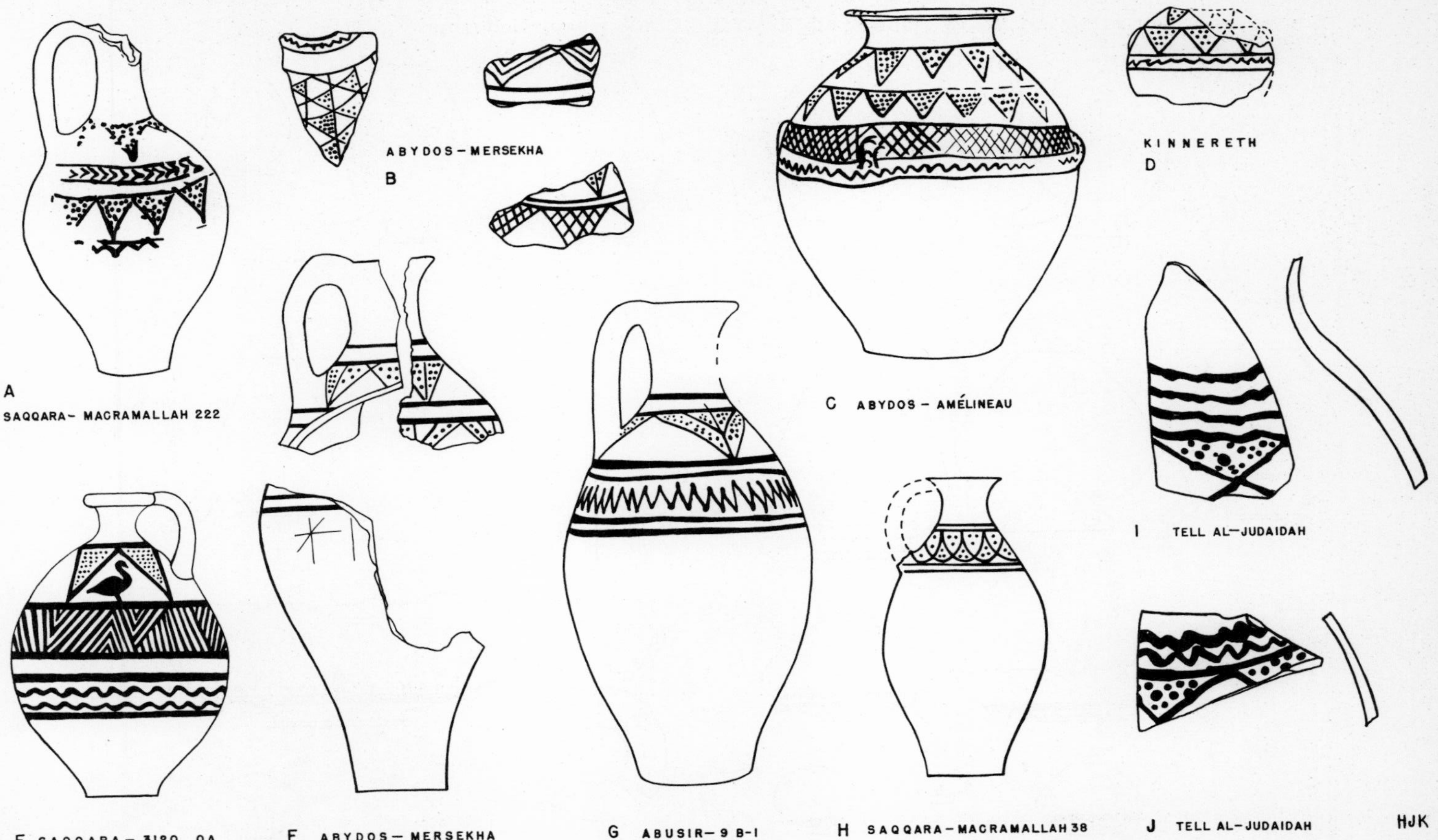

Fig. 3.—Painted Syrian Pottery of the Early Bronze II Period

A SAQQARA—MACRAMALLAH 222

B ABYDOS—MERSEKHA

C ABYDOS—AMÉLINEAU

D KINNERETH

E SAQQARA—3120 QA

F ABYDOS—MERSEKHA

G ABUSIR—9 B·I

H SAQQARA—MACRAMALLAH 38

I TELL AL—JUDAIDAH

J TELL AL—JUDAIDAH

HJK

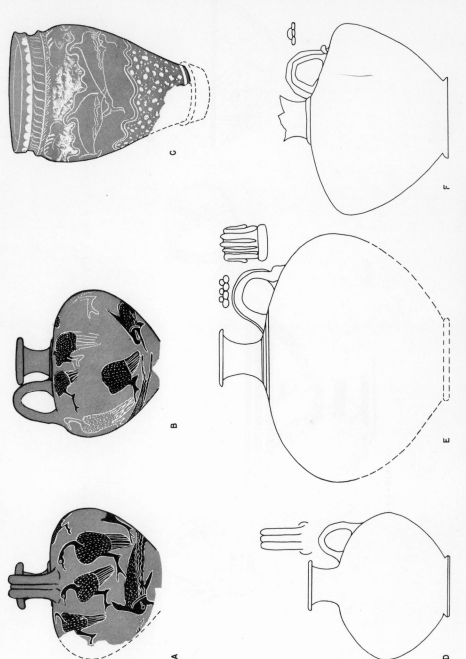

Fig. 4. — A Decorated Jar from Lisht and Related Vessels

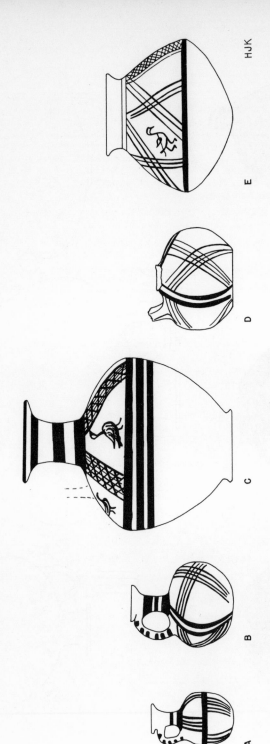

Fig. 5.—Vessels from Egypt Related to the Tell el Ajjul Ware of Late Bronze I

Sources of the Figures

Fig. 1: The Relative Chronology of Egypt and Other Parts
of the Near East through the Middle Bronze Period

The objects and lengths of periods are not to scale. Period names in smaller letters are synchronized on the basis of evidence found outside Egypt and not indicated on this chart. The Palestine-Syria column is divided according to Palestinian and southern Syrian periods, into which the north Syrian (Amuq) phases are inserted. Some references to similar examples from Egypt ("Sim.") and to foreign parallels ("Cf.") are added, but are not intended to be complete.

Abbreviations: ED = Early Dynasty; PL = Protoliterate (PL C-D = Jemdet Nasr; PL A-B = Uruk); S.D. = sequence date; T = tomb; G = grave.

1. Petrie, 1906, Pl. 8B, 101 (Tell el Yahudiyah, G.52).
    Sim.: Ibid., Pl. 8B, 99, 102. Petrie and Brunton, 1924, Pl. 45, 69
    (Sedment). Scharff, 1926, Pl. 76, 4 (Abusir el-Meleq, G.
    48 g 7).
    Cf.: Schaeffer, 1949, pp. 249, Fig. 105, 37; 253, Fig. 107, 28;
    255, Fig. 108, 23. Gjerstad, 1926, p. 72, Jug. 1. Westholm,
    1939, Pls. V, 3, 4; VII, 3, 4.

2. Petrie and Brunton, 1924, Pl. 41, 16 (Sedment, G. 1300).
    Cf.: Loud, 1948, Pl. 26, 17 (Megiddo XII). Schaeffer, 1949, p.
    255, Fig. 108, 19, 20 (Ras Shamra, T. LXXXV).

3. Randall-MacIver and Woolley, 1911, Pl. 49, 10501 (Buhen).
    Cf.: Guiges, 1938, Pl. 3, x, d; p. 44, Fig. 67, z. Ory, 1947-48,
    p. 79, Fig. 7.

4. Petrie and Brunton, 1924, Pl. 45, 67 (Sedment, G. 1262).
    Sim.: Ibid., Pl. 45, 68 (Sedment, G. 1254).
    Cf.: Schaeffer, 1949, p. 253, Fig. 107, 2, 10, 17, 18.

5. Randall-MacIver and Woolley, 1911, Pl. 92, 10864 (Buhen, K 44; red
    polished).
    Sim.: Ibid., Pl. 49. Petrie, 1906, Pl. VIII.
    Cf.: Loud, 1948, Pls. 24, 23 (Megiddo XII); 41, 6 (Megiddo X).

6. Petrie, 1906, Pl. 8, 50 (Tell el Yahudiyah, G. 37).
    See Säve-Söderbergh, 1941, p. 125, n. 5; and S. Smith, 1951, p. 57.

7. Petrie, 1906, Pl. 7, 13 (Tell el Yahudiyah, G. 407).

8. Mace, 1921, p. 17, Fig. 18 (Lisht, Pit 879).

9. Maystre, 1936, p. 682 (Tod deposit of Amenemhet II; silver).

10. Ibid., p. 683 (Tod; Mesopotamian cylinder seal—(Ur III).

11. Engelbach, 1923, Pl. 41, 99D (Harageh, G. 354).

12. Petrie, 1891, Pl. 1, 12 (Kahun town debris).
    Cf.: Evans, 1921, p. 267, Fig. 198.

13. Petrie, 1891, Pl. 1, 13 (Kahun town debris).

14. Vandier, 1937, Pl. 29 (Tod; silver).

15. Ibid.

16. Maystre, 1936, p. 682 (Tod; silver).

17. Evans, 1928, Pl. 9, g (Harageh).

18. Evans, 1921, p. 268, Fig. 199; see also Garstang, 1913, pp. 107-11.
     Cf.: Evans, 1921, p. 268.

19. Reisner, 1942, p. 437, Fig. 256 (Giza 2140A).
     Sim.: Ibid., pp. 467, Fig. 282; 468, Fig. 283; 472, Fig. 285; 476,
           Fig. 287; 489, Fig. 297, a; 509, Fig. 312. Brunton, 1948,
           Pl. 37, 2 (Matmar, G. 3209; Dyn. IV). Jequier, 1929, p. 26,
           Fig. 25 (South Saqqara; Dyn. VI).
     Cf.: Garstang, 1932, Pl. 6, 15-17 (Jericho, T. A). Schaeffer,
           1949, p. 237, Fig. 99, 7, 9 (Ras Shamra III).

20. Reisner, 1942, p. 410, Fig. 234, c (Giza 1233A).

21. Ibid., p. 449, Fig. 274 (Giza 2170A).
     Cf.: Garstang, 1932, Pl. 27, 10 (Jericho, T. A).

22. Reisner, 1942, p. 410, Fig. 234 c, left (Giza 1233).
     Cf.: below, p. 73.

23. Schäfer and Andrae, 1942, p. 254, 2 (Asiatic booty, Mortuary Temple
     of Sahure, Abusir; Dyn. V).

24. Petrie, 1902, Pl. 8, 2 (Abydos, T. of Djer).
     Sim.: Petrie et al., 1925, Pl. 4, 9, 10 (Abydos).
     Cf.: Garstang, 1932, Pl. 2, 11. Garstang, 1935, Pl. 31, 20.

25. Macramallah, 1940, Pl. 46, S4 (Saqqara).
     Sim.: Petrie, 1902, Pl. 8, 8 (Abydos, T. of Djer).
     Cf.: De Vaux and Steve, 1948, p. 555, Fig. 4 (Tell el Fara near
           Nablus). Garstang, 1932, Pls. 12, 8; 20, b.

26. Petrie, 1902, Pl. 8, 2 (Abydos, T. of Djer).
     Sim.: Emery, 1949, p. 153, Fig. 86, G2. Emery, 1938, Pl. 26,
           left. Macramallah, 1940, Pl. 46, S1.
     Cf.: Garstang, 1935, Pl. 27, 24.

27. Petrie, 1902, Pl. 8, 5 (Abydos, T. of Djer).
     Sim.: Ibid., Pl. 8, 4. Petrie et al., 1923, Pl. 53, 97, C, D, E
           (Bashkatib). Emery, 1938, Pl. 26, right. Emery, 1949, p.
           152, Fig. 86, G1. Macramallah, 1940, Pl. 46, S2,3,5,6.
     Cf.: Maisler, 1942, Pl. 1, 39 (Kinnereth; also many
           unpublished examples). Macramallah, 1940, Fig. opp. p.
           70 (Byblos). Engberg and Shipton, 1934, Chart, 11A, 11B.

28. Bonnet, 1928, Pl. 27, middle (Abusir, G. 9 B-1).

29. Macramallah, 1940, Pl. 46, S.

30. Petrie, 1901, Pl. 54 (Abydos, T. of Mersekha).
     Sim.: Petrie, 1902, Pl. 6, 17.
     Cf.: Engberg and Shipton, 1934, Chart, 8C. Garstang, 1935, Pl.
           29, 12, 13.

31. Emery, 1939, Pl. I (Saqqara, plan of elaborately niched, brick mas-
     taba).
     Cf.: Frankfort, 1951, Appendix.

32. Scharff, 1926, Pl. 13, 59 (Abusir el-Meleq, G. 1019; beginning of
     Dyn. I).
     Cf.: Marquet-Krause, 1949, Pls. 71, 774; 72, 824.

33. Menghin, 1934, Pl. 19, c, f (Maadi).
     Cf.: Marquet-Krause, 1949, Pls. 70, 674; 89, 862. Fitzgerald,
           1935, Pl. 5, 26 (Beth Shan XV).

34. Menghin and Amer, 1932, Pl. 34, 2 (Maadi).

35. Menghin, 1934, Pl. 19, c, 5.
    Cf.: Garstang, 1936, Pl. 36, 2 (Jericho VI). Rowe, 1935, Pl. 3.

36. Menghin and Amer, 1932, Pl. 32, 4.

37. Petrie, 1921, Pl. 19, Fancy 99 (Gerzeh; G. 94; S.D. 47-70).
    Cf.: Macalister, 1912, Pl. 44, 2. Sukenik, 1948, Pl. 12, 13.

38. Petrie, 1921, Pl. 28, Wavy 14.

39. Frankfort, 1924, Pl. 13, 1 (ship on jar of the simplified "Decorated" style, British Museum).
    Cf.: Heinrich, 1936, Pl. 17, a.

40. Brunton and Caton-Thompson, 1928, Pl. 40, Decorated 67p (Badari, G. 1728; S.D. 46-57[?]).
    Cf.: Garstang, 1935, Pl. 36, 2 (Jericho VI). Sukenik, 1948, Pl. 12, 14. Vincent, 1911, Pl. 9, 1.

41. Brunton, 1937, Pl. 36, Rough 28 (Mostagedda, G. 11719).
    Sim.: Petrie, 1921, Pl. 13, Polished red 79.

42. Brunton, 1928, Pl. 40, Decorated 59w.

43. Scharff, 1926, Pl. 41, 5 (Abusir el-Meleq, G. 7 g 5).
    Sim.: Petrie, 1921, Pl. 15, Fancy 5a and 5b (Naqada). Brunton, 1937, Pl. 39, 15.
    Cf.: Engberg and Shipton, 1934, Chart, 18A (Megiddo, Stages VII-IV). Fitzgerald, 1935, Pl. 5, 28 (Beth Shan XV). Macalister, 1912, Vol. III, Pl. 48 (Gezer, Cave VII). Sukenik, 1948, Pl. 12, 2. Wampler, 1947, Pl. 52, 1124 (T. 67).

Bowls with conoid projections already begin in the Late Chalcolithic, as at Megiddo and Affulah. Thus it is possible that the Late Chalcolithic period actually overlaps with Late Gerzean. The even correlation here of Early Gerzean with Late Chalcolithic and of Early Bronze I with Late Gerzean may be an oversimplification.

Two examples of such bowls in stone are known, one from an "early deposit" at Megiddo (Engberg and Shipton, 1934, p. 63, Fig. 17) and another from the Step Pyramid complex of Djoser at Saqqara (Lauer, 1939, Pl. 17, 10). The great deposits of stone vessels of the Step Pyramid included examples made in the First Dynasty. The knobbed bowl may be assigned to that period or perhaps even to a slightly earlier time. It was apparently, like the Egyptian one-handled pitchers of stone (Lauer, 1939, Pls. 17, 12; 18, 6; Emery, 1949, p. 144, Fig. 77, DD1), an imitation in stone of a foreign pottery type. The Badarian and Fayum A sherds with small knobs (Brunton, 1937, Pl. 18, Miscellaneous 39, 40; Caton-Thompson and Gardner, 1934, Pl. 17, 24, 25) do not provide Egyptian prototypes for the knobbed bowls, as they are of quite a different character.

44. Petrie, 1921, Pl. 18, Fancy 58K.

45. Brunton, 1937, Pl. 35, Miscellaneous 24.

46. Quibell and Green, 1902, Pl. 28 (from Small Hierakonpolis palette).
    Cf.: Frankfort, 1939, Pls. 4, d, f, h; 5, h. Heinrich, 1936, Pl. 15, i.

47. Capart, 1904, p. 68, Fig. 33 (from gold handle of Gebel Tarif ripple-flaked flint knife).

48. Schäfer and Andrae, 1942, p. 185, 2 (from ivory handle of Gebel el-Arak ripple-flaked flint knife).
     Cf.: Frankfort, 1939, Pl. 4, 1. Heinrich, 1936, Pl. 15, b. Schäfer and Andrae, 1942, p. 471.

49. Kantor, 1952, Pl. 25, B (Naga ed-Der, G. 7304; ca. S.D. 55-60).
     Sim.: Kantor, 1952, p. 243, Fig. 1, A, D, E.
     Cf.: Ibid., Pl. 27. Frankfort, 1939, pp. 292 f.

50. Petrie, 1921, Pl. 28, Wavy 3 (Naqada; S.D. 45, 53).
     Cf.: Engberg and Shipton, 1934, Chart, 12P, 14G, H (Megiddo, Stage VII). Fitzgerald, 1935, Pl. 2, 1-5, 7-9 (Beth Shan XVII-XVI). De Vaux and Steve, 1949, p. 113, Fig. 1, 26 (Tell el Fara, T.3).

51. Petrie, 1921, Pl. 18, Fancy 58a.

52. Ibid., Pl. 18, Fancy 58B.

Fig. 2: Mesopotamian Pottery Types in Prehistoric Egypt
and Palestine

A. Brunton, 1937, Pl. 35, 24 (Mostagedda, G. 1837; no date).

B. Mackay, 1931, Pl. 64, 6 (Jemdet Nasr).

C. Ibid., Pl. 64, 4.

D. Ibid., Pl. 64, 12.

E. Brunton, 1928, Pl. 40, Decorated 59w (Badari, Area 3800; no date).

F. Brunton, 1948, Pl. 12, Decorated 22 (Matmar, G 5112; S.D. 58).

G. De Genouillac et al., 1939, Pl. 25, 2 (Telloh; cf. ibid., p. 35 and Pl. A, bottom).

H. Mackay, 1931, Pl. 64, 3.

I. Petrie, 1921, Pl. 18, Fancy 58K (Diospolis, G. U 187A; S.D. 61).

J. Delougaz, 1952, Pl. 182, C 535.242 (Khafaje; two examples, one PL C, one PL D).

K. Ibid., Pl. 182, C 334.222 (Khafaje: two examples, one PL C, one PL D).

L. Iliffe, 1936, p. 121, No. 63 (Ras el Ain; EB I).

M. Brunton, 1928, Pl. 38, Fancy 581 (Badari, Area 4600; no date).

N. Petrie, 1921, Pl. 18, Fancy 59B (Naqada, G.1619; S.D. 38).

O. Ibid., Pl. 18, Fancy 58a (Naqada, G.1211; not dated; Petrie's range for type is S.D. 40-58).

P. Nöldeke et al., 1932, Pl. 19, B, z (Warka VI; PL A).

Q. Ibid., Pl. 19, B, w (Warka VI; PL A).

R. Ibid., Pl. 19, D, c´ (Warka V; PL B).

S. De Vaux, 1951, p. 584, Fig. 12, 2 (Tell el Fara, T. 12; Late Chalcolithic).

T. Ibid., p. 584, Fig. 12, 4 (Tell el Fara, T. 12; Late Chalcolithic).

Fig. 3: Painted Syrian Pottery of the Early Bronze II Period

A. Macramallah, 1940, Pl. 50, 2 (Saqqara, G. 222).

B. Petrie, 1901, Pl. 54 (Abydos, T. of Mersekha).

C. Amélineau, 1899, Pl. 13, lower row, pot 4 (Abydos, no find spot).

D. Maisler, 1942, Pl. 1, 45 (Kinnereth).

E. Emery, 1949, p. 124, Fig. 68 (Saqqara, Archaic Cemetery, T. 3120; reign of Qa).

F. Petrie, 1901, Pl. 54, top middle (Abydos, T. of Mersekha).

G. Bonnet, 1928, Pl. 27, middle (Abusir, G. 9 B-1).

H. Macramallah, 1940, p. 32, Fig. 28, 5 (Saqqara, T. 38).

I,J. Unpublished sherds from Tell Judaidah illustrated by the permission of Professor R. J. Braidwood.

Fig. 4: A Decorated Jar from Lisht and Related Vessels

A,B. Mace, 1921, p. 17, Fig. 18 (Lisht, Pit 879). I am much indebted to Dr. W. C. Hayes for information concerning Pit 879 and for the photographs from which these drawings were made.

C. Evans, 1921, p. 608, Fig. 477a (Pachyammos).

D. Loud, 1948, Pl. 31, 6 (Megiddo XI).

E. Garstang, 1934, Pl. 21, 13 (Jericho, Palace). Ory, 1947-48, p. 81, Fig. 14 (Dharat el Humaraiya, G 14).

F. Garstang, 1934, Pl. 23, 4 (Jericho, Palace, storeroom 44).

Fig. 5: Vessels from Egypt Related to the Tell el Ajjul
Ware of Late Bronze I

A. Petrie and Brunton, 1924, Pl. 45, 69 (Sedment, G. 1289).
    Cf.: Fig. 1, 1.

B. Ibid., Pl. 45, 70 (Sedment, G. 1289).
    Cf.: Guy, 1938, Pl. 41, 27 (Megiddo, T. 77). Heurtley, 1939, Pl. 8, h (Tell el Ajjul). Westholm, 1939, Pl. 7, 9 (Milia, T. 15).

C. Petrie, 1914, Pl. 9, 25 (Tarkhan, G. 821).

D. Petrie and Brunton, 1924, Pl. 45, 71 (Sedment, G. 1270).
    Cf.: Schaeffer, 1949, p. 233, Fig. 98, 15 (Ras Shamra, T. XXXV). Heurtley, 1939, Pls. 8, d, e, f (Tell el Ajjul); 23, h (Milia).

E. Brunton, 1930, Pl. 16, 55P (Qau, G. 902).

References

Amélineau, E. Les nouvelles fouilles d'Abydos, 1895-1896. Paris, 1899.

Baumgartel, E. J. The Cultures of Prehistoric Egypt, Vol. I. Oxford, 1947.

Bénédite, G. A. "Le Couteau de Gebel el- 'Arak," Commission de la fondation Piot, Monuments et mémoires, XXII (1916), 1-34.

_____. "The Carnarvon Ivory," Journal of Egyptian Archaeology, V (1918), 1-15.

Bonnet, H. Ein frühgeschichtliches Gräberfeld bei Abusir. Leipzig, 1928.

Bono, F. de. "Helouan-El Omari: Fouilles du Service des Antiquités, 1934-1935," Chronique d'Égypte, XXI (1945), 50-54.

_____. "Expédition archéologique royale au désert oriental (Keft-Kosseir): Rapport préliminaire sur la campagne 1949," Annales du Service des Antiquités de l'Égypte, LI (1951), Part I, 59 ff.

Brunton, G. Mostagedda and the Tasian Culture. London, 1937.

_____. Matmar. London, 1948.

Brunton, G., and Caton-Thompson, G. The Badarian Civilization and Pre-dynastic Remains near Badari. London, 1928.

Burton-Brown, T. Studies in Third Millennium History. London, 1946.

_____. Excavations in Azarbaijan, 1948. London, 1948.

Capart, J. Les Débuts de l'art en Égypte. Brussels, 1904.

Caton-Thompson, G., and Gardner, E. W. The Desert Fayum. London, 1934.

Chehab, M. "Tombes phéniciennes, Sin el Fil," Mélanges syriens offert à M. René Dussaud, Vol. II. Paris, 1939.

Delougaz, P. Pottery from the Diyala Region. Chicago, 1952.

Drioton, E., and Vandier, J. Les Peuples de l'Orient méditerranéen, Vol. II: L'Égypte. 3d ed. Paris, 1952.

Dunand, M. Fouilles de Byblos, 1926-1932, Vol. I. Paris, 1939.

Emery, W. B. Excavations at Saqqara: The Tomb of Hemaka. Cairo, 1938.

_____. Excavations at Saqqara, 1937-1938: Hor-Aha. Cairo, 1939.

_____. Great Tombs of the First Dynasty, Vol. I. Cairo, 1949.

Engberg, R. M. The Hyksos Reconsidered. Chicago, 1939.

Engberg, R. M., and Shipton, G. M. Notes on the Chalcolithic and Early Bronze Pottery of Megiddo. Chicago, 1934.

Evans, A. The Palace of Minos, Vol. I. London, 1921.

_____. The Palace of Minos, Vol. II. London, 1928.

_____. The Palace of Minos, Vol. III. London, 1930.

_____. The Palace of Minos, Vol. IV. London, 1935.

Fitzgerald, G. M. "The Earliest Pottery of Beth Shan," The Museum Journal, University Museum, University of Pennsylvania, XXIV (1935), 5-22.

Frankfort, H. Studies in Early Pottery of the Near East. London, 1924.

_____. Cylinder Seals. London, 1939.

_____. The Birth of Civilization in the Near East. Bloomington, Ill., 1951.

Garstang, J. "Note on a Vase of Minoan Fabric from Abydos (Egypt)," Liverpool Annals of Archaeology and Anthropology, V (1913), 107-11.

_____. "Jericho: City and Necropolis, Second Report," ibid., XIX (1932), 3-22.

_____. "Jericho: City and Necropolis, Third Report," ibid., XX (1933), 3-42.

_____. "Jericho: City and Necropolis, Fourth Report," ibid., XXI (1934), 99-136.

_____. "Jericho: City and Necropolis, Sixth Report," ibid., XXIII (1936), 67-100.

Genouillac, H. de, et al. Fouilles de Telloh, Vol. I: Époques présargoniques. Paris, 1934.

Gjerstad, E. Studies on Prehistoric Cyprus. Uppsala, 1926.

Guiges, P. E. "Lébéâ, Kafer-Ǧarra, Qraye: nécropoles de la région sidonienne," Bulletin du Musée de Beyrouth, II (1938), 27-72.

Guy, P. L. O. Megiddo Tombs. Chicago, 1938.

Heinrich, E. Kleinfunde aus den archäischen Tempelschichten in Uruk. ("Ausgrabungen der Deutschen Forschungsgemeinschaft in Uruk-Warka," Vol. I.) Berlin, 1936.

Heurtley, W. A. "A Palestinian Vase Painter of the Sixteenth Century B.C.," Quarterly of the Department of Antiquities in Palestine, VIII (1939), 21-37.

Iliffe, J. H. "Pottery from Ras el ʿAin," Quarterly of the Department of Antiquities in Palestine, V (1936), 113-26.

Jéquier, G. Tombeaux de particuliers contemporaines de Pepi II. Cairo, 1929.

Kantor, H. J. "The Final Phase of Predynastic Culture: Gerzean or Semainean (?)," Journal of Near Eastern Studies, III (1944), 110-36.

_____. Review of Baumgartel (1947) in American Journal of Archaeology, LIII (1949), 76-79.

_____. "Further Evidence for Early Mesopotamian Relations with Egypt," Journal of Near Eastern Studies, XI (1952), 239-50.

Keimer, L. Études de égyptologie, No. VI. Cairo, 1944.

Lauer, J.-P. La Pyramide à degrés, Vol. III: Compléments. Cairo, 1939.

Libby, W. F. Radiocarbon Dating. Chicago, 1952.

Loud, G. Megiddo II: Seasons of 1935-39. Chicago, 1948.

Macalister, R. S. The Excavation of Gezer. London, 1912.

Mace, A. C. "The Egyptian Expedition, 1920-21: Excavations at Lisht," Bulletin of the Metropolitan Museum of Art, XVI, Part II (December, 1921), 5-19.

Mackay, E. Report on Excavations at Jemdet Nasr, Iraq. Chicago, 1931.

Macramallah, R. Un Cimetière archaïque de la classe moyenne du peuple à Saqqarah. Cairo, 1940.

Maisler, B. "An Early Bronze Age Tomb Found at Kinnereth," Bulletin of the Jewish Palestine Exploration Society, Vol. X, No. 1 (1942).

Marquet-Krause, J. Les Fouilles de ʿAy (et-Tell), 1933-1935. Paris, 1949.

Matz, F. Zur ägäischen Chronologie der frühen Bonzezeit," Historia, I (1950), 173-94.

Maystre, C. "A Mysterious 12th-Dynasty Hoard . . . Found at Toud, near Luxor," Illustrated London News, Vol. CLXXXVIII (1936).

Menghin, O., and Amer, M. The Excavations of the Egyptian University in the Neolithic Site at Maadi: First Preliminary Report, Season 1930-31. Cairo, 1932.

Menghin, O. "Die Grabung der Universität Kairo bei Maadi: Drittes Jahrgang," Mitteilungen des Deutschen Instituts für ägyptische Altertumskunde in Kairo, Vol. V (1934).

Nöldeke, A., et al. "Vierter vorläufige Bericht über die von der Notgemeinschaft der Deutschen Wissenschaft in Uruk unternommenen Ausgrabungen (1931-32)," Abhandlungen der Preussischen Akademie der Wissenschaften, Phil-hist. Kl., No. 6, Jahrgang 1932.

Ory, J. A Bronze-Age Cemetery at Dhahrat el Humraiya," Quarterly of the Department of Antiquities in Palestine, XIII (1947-48), 75-91.

Quibell, J. E., and Green, F. W. Hierakonpolis II. London, 1902.

Parker, R. A. The Calendars of Ancient Egypt. Chicago, 1950.

Pendlebury, J. D. S. Aegyptiaca: A Catalogue of Egyptian Objects in the Aegean Area. Cambridge, 1930.

_____. The Archaeology of Crete. London, 1939.

Petrie, F. Illahun, Kahun, and Gurob 1889-1890. London, 1891.

_____. The Royal Tombs of the First Dynasty, Vol. II. London, 1901.

_____. Abydos I. London, 1902.

_____. Hyksos and Israelite Cities. London, 1906.

_____. Tarkhan II. London, 1914.

_____. Corpus of Prehistoric Pottery and Palettes. London, 1921.

Petrie, F., and Brunton, G. Sedment I. London, 1924.

Petrie, F., et al. The Labyrinth, Gerzeh, and Mazghuneh. London, 1912.

_____. Lahun II. London, 1923.

_____. Tombs of the Courtiers and Oxyrhynkhos. London, 1925.

Porter, B.; Moss, R. L. B.; and Burney, E. W. Topographical Bibliography of Egyptian Hieroglyphic Texts, Reliefs, and Paintings, Vol. VII: Nubia, the Deserts, and Outside Egypt. Oxford, 1951.

Randall-MacIver, P., and Woolley, C. L. Buhen. Philadelphia, 1911.

Reisner, G. A. A History of the Giza Necropolis, Vol. I. Cambridge, Mass., 1942.

Roque, Bisson de la. Trésor de Tôd ("Catalogue Général du Musée du Caire.") Cairo, 1950.

Rowe, A. "The 1934 Excavations at Gezer," Palestine Exploration Fund Quarterly Statement (1935), pp. 19-33.

Säve-Söderbergh, T. Ägypten und Nubien. Lund, 1941.

_____. "The Hyksos Rule in Egypt," Journal of Egyptian Archaeology, Vol. XXXVII (1951).

Schäfer, H., and Andrae, W. Die Kunst des alten Orients. 3d ed. Berlin, 1942.

Schaeffer, C. F. L. Ugaritica II. Paris, 1949.

Scharff, A. Das vorgeschichtliche Gräberfeld von Abusir el-Meleq. Leipzig, 1926.

Smith, S. "Middle Minoan I-II and Babylonian Chronology," American Journal of Archaeology, XLIX (1945), 1-24.

Smith, W. S. Ancient Egypt as Represented in the Museum of Fine Arts, Boston. 3d ed. Boston, 1952.

Sukenik, E. L. Archaeological Excavations at ʿAffula Conducted on Behalf of the Hebrew University. Jerusalem, 1948.

Vandier, J. "A propos d'un dépôt de provenance asiatique trouvé à Tod," Syria, XVIII (1937), 174-82.

Vaux, R. de. "La troisième campagne de fouilles à Tell el-Farʿah près Naplouse," Revue biblique, LVI (1949), 102-38.

Vaux, R. de, and Steve, A. M. "La deuxième campagne de fouilles à Tell el-Farʿah, près Naplouse," Revue biblique, LV (1948), 544-80.

Vincent, P. Underground Jerusalem: Discoveries on the Hill of Ophel (1909-11). London, 1911.

Wampler, J. C. Tell en Naṣbeh, Vol. II: The Pottery. Berkeley and New Haven, 1947.

Westholm, A. "Some Late Cypriote Tombs at Milia," Quarterly of the Department of Antiquities of Palestine, VIII (1939), 1-20.

Winkler, H. A. Rock-Drawings of Southern Upper Egypt, Vol. I. London, 1938.

A Survey of the Archeological Chronology
of Palestine from Neolithic to Middle Bronze

W. F. Albright
Johns Hopkins University

During the five years that have elapsed since completion of the manuscript of the writer's book The Archaeology of Palestine (Pelican Books,
1949), the work interrupted by the war has begun again with redoubled vig-
or. Among the relevant publications of the last five years may be mentioned particularly the following (listed according to their chronological
relation to our subject): René Neuville's posthumous work, Le Paléo-
lithique et le mésolithique du Désert de Judée (1951); M. Stekelis' descrip-
tions of his work in the Yarmukian of Sha'ar ha-Golan, published since
1950;[1] Nelson Glueck's Explorations in Eastern Palestine, Vol. IV (1951);
Megiddo II (1948); R. de Vaux's reports on his excavations at Tell el-
Far'ah northeast of Nablus (in the Revue biblique, 1947-51); Judith Marquet-Krause, Les Fouilles de 'Ay (et-Tell) 1933-1935 (1949); Kathleen
Kenyon's work at Jericho since 1952 (published in various preliminary
accounts by Miss Kenyon and A. Douglas Tushingham).

Fundamental to any chronological treatment of the earlier periods
are the radiocarbon counts, which are now available for a few key assemblages of Mesopotamia and Egypt, though none has hitherto been reported
for early Palestine. Particularly significant are the datings for the latest
pre-pottery Neolithic (Qal'at Jarmo) of the eastern Tigris country, within
a century or two of an average date about 4750 B.C., and for the earliest-
known pottery Neolithic of Egypt (Fayum A), within a range of three centuries or so, centering about 4250 B.C. This would suggest a date for the
introduction of pottery in the second quarter of the fifth millennium. In
the first printing of his Archaeology of Palestine (Pelican ed.), p. 61, the
writer dated the introduction of the art of making pottery in Palestine "before 5000 B.C." This date would now have to be lowered to "after 5000

---

1. See especially his paper, "A New Neolithic Industry: The Yarmukian
    of Palestine," Israel Exploration Journal, I, 1-19; as well as his more
    recent Hebrew survey, "The Neolithic Period in Palestine," Bulletin
    of the Israel Exploration Society, XVII (1952), 21-25.

B.C. at the earliest, and probably in the second quarter of the fifth millennium." Other dates would have to be reduced correspondingly. The end of the Mesolithic would probably have to be brought down to the middle of the sixth millennium.[2] The pre-pottery Neolithic Jericho of Garstang (layers X—XVII) and Miss Kenyon belongs to the first half of the fifth millennium, while the pottery Neolithic of Jericho IX and the related Yarmukian of northern Palestine should be dated between ca. 4500 and 4000. Jericho VIII and the lowest level of Tell el-Farʿah, with contemporary settlements elsewhere, should be dated between ca. 4200 and 3700 (highest and lowest dates, respectively).[3] Similarly, we should date the Ghassulian period not earlier than ca. 3800 and not later than ca. 3400 B.C.[4] The typologically later deposits of Beth-shan XVII and the Jericho area belong somewhere between ca. 3500 and 3300 B.C. The Esdraelon phase falls between ca. 3400 and 3100 B.C. We may expect fluctuation in details for a long time to come, unless new and even more powerful controls are discovered by physical or biological scientists. Our present confidence would have been regarded as foolhardy five years ago.

Dr. Kantor's admirable survey of the correlations between the ceramic chronology of Egypt and Palestine will be presupposed throughout this paper, which consists mainly of some footnotes to her presentation.

2. The dates proposed by Stekelis before radiocarbon had transformed the picture (op. cit., p. 19) are much too high. It is unlikely that the end of the Mesolithic is to be dated much before ca. 5500 B.C. (instead of about 8000 B.C.), and the beginning of the Ghassulian can scarcely be placed before the thirty-eighth century B.C.

3. See the Hebrew survey of the Neolithic and Chalcolithic of Palestine, with an excellent chart, by Ruth Amiran (Bulletin of the Israel Exploration Society, XVII, 12-21), where Jericho VIII and its congeners are correctly placed; cf. also my Archaeology of Palestine (Pelican ed.), p. 66.

4. Maurice Dunand has tried to prove that the Ghassulian period (specifically, the last stratum, which is the only one we know in detail) has been erroneously dated by all recent Palestinian archeologists and that it should actually be regarded as contemporary with Early Bronze I and II and dated at the beginning of the third millennium. The Esdraelon culture he considers exclusively local. He naturally disregards Sukenik's discovery of Ghassulian remains at ʿAffuleh under a floor of the Esdraelon period (Archaeological Investigations at ʿAffula, [Jerusalem, 1948], p. 17). These remains included a bird-vase of characteristically Ghassulian type (see on it the admirable article by Ruth Amiran, in Bulletin of the American Schools of Oriental Research, No. 130 [1953], pp. 11-14). Furthermore, Dunand's argument is based almost wholly on analogies—architectural as well as ceramic—with Syria and Mesopotamia, whereas he entirely disregards the rich material now available for sequence-dating of Chalcolithic pottery and flints within Palestine itself.

Her caution in not giving any absolute dates is praiseworthy, but no longer necessary. We are now safe in approximating the chronology of Scharff
and Stock, from which the independent chronology, defended by the writer
since 1925, seldom diverges by over fifty years.[5] The dates which I have
given since 1934 are based on this chronology, which can scarcely be ap-
preciably wrong for the successive phases of Early Bronze.

The foreign pottery found by Dr. Mustapha Amer at Ma ʿadeh (Archaeology of Palestine [Pelican ed.], p. 70) is characterized by smooth ledge
handles and high loop handles. There can be no doubt that it fits best into
the picture presented by the early part of the Esdraelon culture of Palestine—say between ca. 3400 (earliest possible date) and 3200 (latest possible date). This agrees very well with the fact that the archeologists with
whom I discussed the date of Maʿadeh in Egypt (1947-51) all equated it
roughly with the Early and Middle Gerzean. As is well known from the
work of Wright, Late Gerzean is roughly parallel with Early Bronze I in
Palestine; the latter follows immediately after the Esdraelon phase and
seems to overlap it.

Miss Kantor has called attention to the apparent absence of Palestinian pottery from Egyptian sites of the Second and Third Dynasties. As
she suggests, this is probably due to lack of sufficient archeological data
from these dynasties in Egypt itself. There can be no doubt that Egypt
continued to exercise a strong influence over its Asiatic satellites through
the late Thinite and early Memphite periods. She has mentioned the find
of a fragment of a stone vessel bearing the name of the last king of the
Second Dynasty (Khasekhemwey) at Byblos (see p. 9 above). But there
is more material. At Ai (et-Tell) in central Palestine, Mme Marquet-
Krause discovered a considerable number of calcite trays and basins
(large bowls), which had been imported into Palestine during the Second
and Third Dynasties, as proved by their shapes, which resemble similar
objects from the time of Binothris of the Second and Djoser of the Third
very closely.[6] That they were highly prized is proved by the fact that
they were still kept in a sanctuary of EB III. The writer has also called

5. See for these dates Hanns Stock's Studia Aegyptiaca II ("Analecta Ori-
    entalia," Vol. XXXI [Rome, 1949]), p. 103; and the writer's review,
    Bulletin of the American Schools of Oriental Research, No. 119 (Oc-
    tober, 1950), p. 29.
6. See the writer's observations, Journal of the Palestine Oriental Soci-
    ety, XV (1935), 209 f.; and Judith Marquet-Krause, Les Fouilles de
    ʿAy (et-Tell), p. 19.

attention to the fact that the construction of a Canaanite tomb of about EB II closely resembles similar Egyptian work from the time of Djoser in important respects.[7] Since we are already in complete agreement with regard to the chronological relation between the First Dynasty and EB II, as well as between the Fourth-Sixth Dynasties and EB III, this would mean that there were continued cultural relations between Egypt and Palestine from Early Gerzean until the end of the Old Kingdom. If it were not for the fact that the temples and palaces of Early Bronze are mostly buried deep under still unexplored mounds, we should undoubtedly have much more direct evidence of Egyptian influence on Palestine in the third millennium.

In spite of the absence of direct correlations between Egyptian and Palestinian archeological material from the period beginning with the latter part of the Sixth Dynasty and ending in the latter part of the Twelfth Dynasty (ca. 2200-1850 B.C.), there can be no doubt about the chronological situation. The latter part of EB III may be called EB IIIB (Wright, second phase) or EB IV (Wright, first phase); there can be no doubt that it is substantially a continuation of EB IIIA, with increasingly slovenly ware. The following transitional phase, with "envelope handles," is well represented at Tell Beit Mirsim and Megiddo, as well as at numerous other sites on both sides of the Jordan; it must certainly be dated between the twenty-second century (earliest possible date) and the twentieth (latest possible date). The following period of "caliciform" pottery (Tell Beit Mirsim H) is very well represented in different parts of Palestine; it forms a stratigraphic interlude between the phase characterized by envelope handles and the first phase of Middle Bronze II=Tell Beit Mirsim G-F and Megiddo XIV-XIII (overlapping stratigraphically with pottery attributed to XV, otherwise equivalent to Tell Beit Mirsim H; and Megiddo XII, otherwise=Tell Beit Mirsim E).[8]

We are handicapped in establishing correlations for these phases outside Palestine because of the fact that little has yet appeared in published

---

7. Bulletin of the American Schools of Oriental Research, No. 94 (1944), pp. 14 ff.
8. Cf. my Archaeology of Palestine (Pelican ed.), pp. 80 ff. Not yet antiquated are the treatments of the material by G. E. Wright (Bulletin of the American Schools of Oriental Research, No. 71, pp. 27-34) and in part by myself (Bulletin of the American Schools of Oriental Research, No. 95, pp. 3-11), dealing with the chronological background. I should still indorse virtually everything which we wrote in 1938 and 1944.

form. After the publication of Braidwood's material from Tell Judeideh and Woolley's from Alalakh, after the publication of the Hamath series in more complete form, and after Maurice Dunand has published his stratigraphic data from Byblos, including selections from his vast accumulation of pottery, we shall see more clearly. Meanwhile, we can merely mark time, confident only that there will not be any appreciable modification of the chronological scheme already established.

For the same reason, we encounter difficulties in correlating the MB II sequence in Palestine and Phoenicia with that farther north and east. If the pottery series from Mari and Alalakh were published, we should certainly have little difficulty in setting up convincing parallels. In particular, we should make the Khabur ware of the Euphrates Valley, first identified and dated stratigraphically by Mallowan, roughly contemporary with MB IIA (Megiddo XIV-XIII=Tell Beit Mirsim G-F). The latter is known to have come into use by the time of the royal tombs of Byblos contemporary with Amenemmes III and IV (late nineteenth and early eighteenth centuries B.C.); it lasted until somewhere in the second half of the eighteenth century in Palestine, but the Khabur phase may naturally have lasted longer (cf. Ann Perkins, pp. 50-51, below).

Here our chronology is dislocated for the time being by the prevailing tendency to follow Sidney Smith's Mesopotamian chronology (some 64 years higher than my dates since 1942) or even Albrecht Goetze's present system (about 120 years higher than mine).[9] There can be no doubt that the Tod deposit, with its seal cylinders of Ur III type, favors the low chronology which I follow, since the deposit in question can be dated somewhere in or near the last quarter of the twentieth century B.C. (reign of Amenemmes II); but this does not constitute proof. Radiocarbon has been tried, but it does not provide sufficiently precise dates to decide a controversy which moves within outside limits of a century or so.

The only point in Miss Kantor's paper where I should dissent from her conclusions is her treatment of the chronology of Middle Minoan. She is obviously correct in pointing out a relationship between the plain or torsional fluting of the silver bowls from the Tod deposit and similar designs on Kamares ware of Middle Minoan IIA, as well as in saying that the pottery styles were derived from metallic ornament. However, there

---

9. Cf. most recently the debate between Rowton, Goetze, and myself, Bulletin of the American Schools of Oriental Research, Nos. 126, pp. 20-26, and 127, pp. 21-30.

is sometimes striking disparity between the development of decorative
motifs in different mediums and in different crafts. Moreover, metallic
objects lasted so much longer than pottery objects that they are far less
reliable as a basis for dating. If the use of these fluted designs continued
generations after the attestation of them at Tod, it is perfectly possible
that MM II did not begin for a good century after the Tod deposit was made.
There is no proof that Kamares ware was imported into Egypt until the
last decades of the Twelfth Dynasty. There is no a priori reason why MM
IIA and B should have lasted longer than a century and a half together.[10]
At present there is a dearth of clear-cut stratigraphic evidence for both
sequence dating and absolute chronology of Middle Minoan, but one sus-
pects that complete publication of the sites recently excavated in Syria
would go a long way toward clearing up this, as well as other, chronological problems of the first half of the second millennium B.C. Meanwhile,
Palestinian dates, very well established relatively, and solidly pegged
down at key points by the astronomically fixed chronology of contemporary Egypt, form the only reliable pivots in our system of southwest-
Asiatic archeology in the Middle Bronze Age.

---

10. Cf. also my remarks, Bibliotheca orientalis, V (1948), 126. It has
since, however, been observed by Aegean archeologists that Tholos
B in the Cretan Mesará cannot be used with any confidence for chronological correlations because of its mixed content, which seems to
cover two centuries or more.

A Tentative Relative Chronology of Syria from the
Terminal Food-gathering Stage to ca. 2000 B.C.
(Based on the Amouq Sequence)

Robert J. Braidwood
University of Chicago

Geographical Considerations

The area referred to here as "Syria" includes the modern states of
Lebanon, Syria (excluding those portions east of the Euphrates drainage),
Hatay (the ex-Sandjak of Alexandretta), and Turkish Mesopotamia (below
the ca. 2,500-foot contour). Save for the high woodland elevations of the
Lebanon-Anti-Lebanon chain, three natural areas are involved: (1) the
coastal strip, characterized by Mediterranean vegetation and relatively
heavy winter rains; (2) the Irano-Turanian grassland to open-woodland
vegetation, with ca. 10 - 25 inches of winter rainfall; and (3) the Saharo-
Sindian desert-vegetation hinterland, with less than 10 inches of annual
rainfall (Fisher, 1950, Fig. 16 and folder II). The third vegetation zone
is of no concern to us except for such sites as Baghouz and Mari, which
lie along the mud flats of the Euphrates.

The first and second natural areas extend without interruption into
Palestine and into Iraq, but the archeological assemblages of these two
adjoining regions tend to vary—to a more or less marked degree—from
those of Syria, even from the time of the earliest village materials now
in hand.

The earliest available village materials seem already to reflect the
two important natural areas, the Mediterranean coastal and the Irano-
Turanian grasslands on the inner slopes of the folded zone. The assemblage seen first in Amouq A and the lower Mersin "neolithic," characterized by dark-faced burnished pottery, seems to have its focus in Syro-
Cilicia; as one moves south, the catalogue changes gradually, and we suspect that a somewhat variant, although possibly related, coastal Palestinian assemblage will eventually be delineated (Braidwood and Braidwood,
1953, p. 288). The earliest available village materials of the grasslands
of the Euphrates-Khabur drainage reflect—in the suggestions of a "pre-
Halaf" assemblage now in hand—a zone of cultural contact or fusion, half

Syro-Cilician, half Hassunan. The focus of the Hassunan development would seem itself to have been in the Tigris drainage area. Comparably early village materials are not yet available from inland southern Syria; but we would expect the area to have originally supported a northerly variant of the inland Palestine assemblage, now being delineated so competently at Jericho by Kathleen Kenyon.

This geographico-cultural duality—coastland versus inland and north versus south—remains characteristic of Syria throughout its later prehistory and early history. This is not to say that the cultural foci were ever isolated, however, as there are traces of interchange of traits almost from the very beginning and in increasing strength as time passes.

One further geographical point: Syria (or at least its more northerly portions) must have been an integral part of "nuclear" western Asia, as regards the beginnings of food production. I would be very much surprised if assemblages technologically and chronologically similar to Jarmo (and Jarmo's antecedents) will not yet be discovered in Syria. Jericho already represents such a case farther to the south and inland; the general technological equivalence with Jarmo is marked, but the time may prove to be slightly later.

Present Status of Archeological Knowledge

The available materials for the time range of our interest are, in the main, grossly inadequate and have been treated selectively (especially where painted pottery happens to have been included). There has been little attention to the potential variety of categories in the successive assemblages, to quantitative treatment in general, or to the nonartifactual types of evidence. In only two or three cases have sites been consciously selected for their prehistoric or early historic content alone, thus allowing adequate architectural exposures of these levels.

1. Pleistocene prehistory.—Only enough is known of the materials of the terminal era of the food-gathering stage to assure that they existed in the area. The Yabrud and Ksar Akil sequences are the important excavated occurrences, but neither are particularly clear in the strictly "terminal" range. The Nebekian of Yabrud includes spiky-pointed microliths probably related to the Kebaran of Palestine; this is followed by a rather Natufian-like industry (probably latish) with crescents and Helwan retouch. Finally, Yabrud had a "neolithic" upper stratum which did not yield many artifacts and which is not very comprehensible.

In a cave adjacent to Ksar Akil (which did not itself run as late as the Nebekian of Yabrud), there was a disturbed layer which evidently once had a "terminal" sort of microlithic industry. Other random finds—mainly surface—near Beyrouth have yielded a variety of microlithic implements, of which some may be Natufian-like; the same situation probably obtains near Damascus. Otherwise, the strictly terminal era of the food-gathering stage is unreported.

2. The sequence from the earliest now available village-farmer sites onward—ordered in terms of the Amouq sequence.—(I must apologize for basing myself primarily on the still unpublished Amouq materials, the completed manuscript of the earlier materials of which will be published by the University of Chicago Press in 1954-55. The Oriental Institute's excavations in the Amouq did yield the only essentially complete sequence so far available, however. It was controlled with some respect to the quantitative frequency of the major categories, and the exposures—while never really large—were relatively adequate. The alphabetic nomenclature, which differs from my old Judaidah "period" nomenclature [Braidwood, 1937, pp. 6-7], is to be found in Krogman [1949], Table I).

The materials of this range, with the exception of at least one cave and several cemetery situations, come from mounds. It is extremely unlikely that we have to deal here with an antiquity greater than ca. 4500 B.C., and the sequence is not considered in any detail after ca. 2000 B.C. There is no radioactive carbon dating yet available from most of the area. On comparative typological grounds, the Amouq G materials show certain convincing equivalences with items in the later part of the Protoliterate and of Early Dynastic I in Mesopotamia. In the south it will probably be possible (with the appearance of Fouilles de Byblos, Vol. II) to fix some of the Byblos "Early Bronze" materials as definitely earlier than the first Egyptian dynasty. The single available C^{14} date in the area is for the "First Urban Installation" of Byblos and is 3364 B.C. $\pm$ 300 years. From this time onward, the order of imprecision of dating is probably slightly less than $\pm$ 200 years.

Figure 1 suggests the succession of assemblages involved; the objects sketched and the pottery and flint sequence suggested are based on the Amouq sites.

Phase A.—Only in the case of Byblos "A" is there much architectural information (other occurrences being either too restricted or below groundwater); this Byblos evidence being for small, more or less rectangular room-floors made of a sort of lime plaster. The most characteristic ceramic element of the phase is a dark-faced burnished ware, save in the south where a mat-impressed or incised ware occurs (along with normal dark-faced burnished ware). The flint industry of the south resembles that of Palestine; that of the north is unique and characteristic and includes projectile points and short, snapped sickle blades. In the Amouq, full-ground celts, whorls, stamp seals, and vessels of stone are available.

The clearest occurrences are so far known along the coastal strip; partially similar assemblages are known to have existed at Halaf and Carchemish, but these already show traces of Hassunan contact, in so far as they are understood in detail.

Phase B.—Essentially, this is a continuation of the Phase A type of assemblage; some local development in pottery occurs, also the appearance of Hassunan-inspired incised ware and possibly of Hassunan painted ware is noted. The range was not complete in the Amouq exposure—it can be seen best in its later aspect at Mersin.

Phase C.—The basic A-B ceramic tradition is continued, but a certain amount of influence of the Halafian painted-pottery tradition is felt (sherds in non-Amouq clays with Halafian motifs make up ca. 5 per cent of the total bulk), and Halaf painting and profiles are imitated locally. A new (and not otherwise described) flint industry appears. The earliest clay "sling missiles" occur now (these are certainly earlier in the Hassunan focus), and flint or obsidian projectile points are no longer importantly present. This phase will doubtless be seen to have graded typologically into "classic" Halafian as one moves eastward into the hinterland. It is noteworthy that H. Schmidt believes that dark-faced burnished ware exists with Halaf pottery in the type site itself.

Phase D.—In ceramics this is a phase of adaptation by the local potters of both the indigenous and the borrowed wares into several peculiar local products. The first firm ceramic links with Palestine (e.g., Jericho VIII) now occur. This phase is hinted at but is not so far described outside the Amouq, where its exposure is very small—it badly needs further delineation. In the coastal sites (e.g., Ras Shamra IV) this range will doubtless be parallel to, but somewhat different from, the transitional Halafian-Ubaidian range of northerly Iraq, upper Khabur, etc.

Phase E.—The last traces of the old dark-faced burnished-ware tradition are now finally submerged by a full-scale appearance of a northerly variant of the Ubaidian painted-pottery style and its associated simple and cooking wares. Nevertheless, the available assemblage is by no means the exact equivalent of a northerly Iraq Ubaidian one. The range was not complete in our Amouq exposures, although we isolated later material on surface sites. This later aspect may now be seen on Tell es-Sheik, where I suspect that the zone of contact to Phase F will be evident (as it is in Mersin and Tarsus).

Phase F.—Lacking the zone of contact between Phases E and F, with the gray burnished wares of "Gawran" type (which appear at Tell es-Sheik, Tarsus, and Mersin), the clear break between the phases may be more apparent than real. Nevertheless, the several ceramic wares are now quite different from anything seen earlier, and it is probable that some sort of "potter's wheel" was now in use. The first well-attested mud-brick structures are available in the coastal zone (mud brick was evidently earlier in the hinterland), a new flint industry (mainly blades of the type called "Canaanean") appears, and there is a rather well-developed industry in metal. The phase is not at all well delineated in the hinterland west of the Iraqi border; on the south coast it is probable that Byblos "enéolithique 'B'" is some sort of southern variant of the phase.

It seems likely that this assemblage is rather closely related to the

Gawran of northerly Iraq; both may yet be found to derive from a focus in the hilly flanks of Turkish Mesopotamia.

Phase G.—This is a "new" assemblage; but a break with certain ceramic and metal industries of F is not clear, and the F flint industry continues. "Reserved-slip" ware, incised ware, cylinder seals, fluted mace heads, and a variety of amulets link to late Protoliterate southerly Iraq; the "Syrian bottles"—in both their simple and painted forms—link to Palestine and the Abydos tombs (1st Dyn. Egypt). But, unfortunately, a neat synchronism is not possible to the south, as these "bottles" tend to persist into Phase H (cf. H. J. Kantor, p. 9 above). Phase G seems to have been a phase of considerable activity and even brilliance; unfortunately, it is practically unexamined west of the Euphrates, save in the Amouq. Brak E would be a good eastern example of the phase.

Phase H.—This is marked by the appearance of two wares known to have more northerly counterparts (red-black ware, the so-called "Khirbet Kerak ware"; brittle orange ware), certain secondary architectural features (hearths with "andirons," benches, etc.), also apparently northern in origin, and some items in metal which are at least known to have occurred also in the north. Mesopotamian-type cylinder seals still occur, and the "Syrian bottles" are present in the earlier aspect of Phase H (cf. H. J. Kantor, p. 9 above). Essentially, Phase H shows a continuation of the major Phase G items, with the northern elements added over and above those of the G assemblage. This situation seems not to obtain east of the Orontes Valley (i.e., it is essentially a coastal situation). The easily recognizable red-black ("Khirbet Kerak") ware has not been noticed on any site of the Euphrates drainage. Presumably, the transition from the major ceramic traditions of Phase G to Phase I type (which is suggested but not fully delineated in the Amouq) took place in the Euphrates drainage. At some time late in Phase H or early Phase I there was a strong contact with Palestine, which carried the "Khirbet Kerak" ware southward.

Phase I.—In the Amouq the new northern elements of Phase H are continued, but the Phase G ceramic is replaced by a factory-made simple-surfaced series which include goblets, and which has been called the "caliciform pottery" by Albright and others. It is this ceramic which may have been developed out of the older Phase G simple-ware tradition in the Euphrates drainage. This is the basic ceramic of the large tomb at Til Barsib on the Euphrates, which also included a fine selection of metal.

Phase J.—Phase J in the Amouq is marked by refinements in the ceramic of Phase I type, by somewhat more painted ware (including an incision through paint, of goblets and small jars), and by the disappearance of the northern wares of Phase H. The metals of Til Barsib type, the Troy IV cup, and metal molds indicate how this phase is part of the general widespread interlinking of the end of the third millennium B.C. (cf. Hissar III, Alaca tombs, Troy, etc.).

The regularity of the ceramic industry over the general Syrian area (with the possible exception of the extremes of the area—e.g., Byblos and Chagar Bazar?) is marked. The "factory-made" feel of most of the pottery and metals is noticeable, and the industrial traditions for most of the indigenous products of the earlier 2nd millennium are now apparently set.

. . . .

Phase J probably ends about 2000 B.C., by which time Syria—especially along the coast—is already becoming a focus of the activity which

Breasted termed "the first great internationalism." One very soon has to deal with sites which are of literate and urban establishments (Atchana, Byblos, Ras Shamra, and Mari on the Euphrates are cases in point). The artifactual manifestations of this "internationalism" are too complex to examine here. George Hanfmann's review of Schaeffer's Stratigraphie comparée (1951, 1952), suggests what is involved. This internationalism —in its Syrian aspect—was a growth out of the cultural soil of which the assemblages of Phases I and J are an archeological expression.

References

Braidwood, Robert J. Mounds in the Plain of Antioch: An Archaeological Survey. Chicago, 1937.

Braidwood, Robert J. and Linda. "The Earliest Village Communities of Southwest Asia," Journal of World History, I (1953), 278-310.

Fisher, W. B. The Middle East. London: Methuen, 1950.

Hanfmann, George. Review of Stratigraphie comparée by Claude Schaeffer, American Journal of Archaeology, LV (1951), 355-65 and LVI (1952), 27-32.

Krogman, W. M. "Ancient Cranial Types," Belleten Türk Tarih Kurumu, XIII (1949), 407-77.

Chronological correlation chart (hand-drawn)

Column headings (left to right): EGYPT · PALEST. · AMOUQ — POTTERY — FLINT — GENERAL · OTHER SYRIAN & SYRO-CILICIAN SITES · MESPOT. · N.W.

MESPOT. / N.W. (right columns):
- TROY IV
- AGADE
- GAWRA 6
- CHALER 2–3
- BRAK C–D
- E.D. III
- E.D. II
- NINEVITE
- E.D. I
- ALISHAR "copper" ?
- P.L. d
- BRAK E
- P.L. c — NINEVEH II
- P.L. b
- P.L. a "chal." ?
- GAWRA

OTHER SYRIAN & SYRO-CILICIAN SITES:
- SIMIRIYAN
- HAMA J (III–IV) — Sheikhoun, Qatna — CARCHEMISH Hammam, etc.
- TARSUS 8–10.5 m.
- TIL BARSIB tombs
- HAMA J (I–II) — ASSAN, AS, MASIN, QATNA, etc.
- SUKAS
- SINDJIRLE
- SUKAS
- HAMA K (upper)
- TARSUS
- RAS SHAMRA III
- MERSIN ca. XII
- HAMA K
- QALAT ER-RUS 16–12
- SIMIRIYAN
- BYBLOS — Lebea, tomb 6
- QALAT ER-RUS 19–16 — CARCHEMISH
- BYBLOS "énéolithique B" — CARCHEMISH
- HAMA K
- MERSIN ca. XIV–XIII — GAWRA (?)

AMOUQ phases (pottery types band):
FLINTS — F and following types

Pottery / type labels:
- COMB-IMP.
- BRITTLE-ORANGE
- SMEARED-WASH
- SIMPLE
- COARSE
- RED-BLACK
- GREY
- SIMPLE
- BEVEL-RIM
- PAINTED
- SYRIAN BOTTLES
- SPIRAL
- PAINTED GOBLETS
- INCISED DEC.
- DOUBLE-SLIP
- SIMPLE
- MULTIPLE BRUSH
- CORRUGATED
- RESERVED-SLIP
- COARSE RED

Amouq phase letters: K · J · I · H · G · F · A

EGYPT / PALEST.:
- M.B.I
- 6TH DYN. (III–B)
- 5TH DYN.
- 4TH DYN. — E.B.III
- 3RD DYN.
- 2ND DYN.
- E.B.II
- 1ST DYN. Late
- B. — E.B.I
- GERZEAN
- Early
- ESDRAELON

Cylinder / seal notations: CYLINDERS E.D.III · CYLINDERS E.D. I & II Proto-Lit. D · CYLINDERS Proto-Lit. · STAMPS geometric & animal motifs · Anakis, Beads, Pierce, Glass, Turquoise · Stone & flint · Pins · Mould

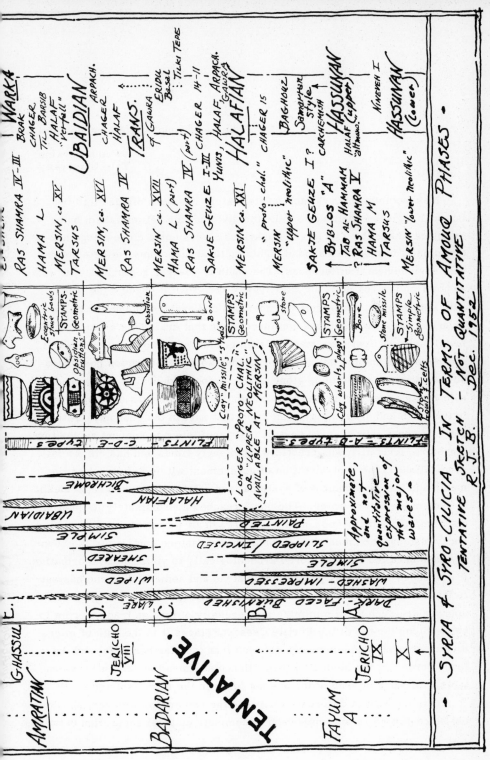

Figure 1

The Relative Chronology of Mesopotamia

Ann Perkins
Yale University

Mesopotamia through most of its history has been divided into two
cultural regions—north and south—the dividing line between them being
the place where the Tigris and Euphrates rivers come closest together in
the vicinity of modern Baghdad. This cultural dichotomy reflects noticeable environmental differences. The south is younger geologically; it was
an arm of the sea until the Pleistocene age, when it began to be filled
with silts brought down from the northern and eastern mountains by the
rivers, a process which has continued since that era. This created an al-
luvial plain, at first very marshy, then gradually drying out as more silt
was deposited and the delta pushed farther south. The region possesses
no good timber, no building stone, and no mineral deposits; hence trade
with regions possessing these desirable commodities was developed early
in the south and always played an important part in the economy. Although
there is some rain in early spring, it is insufficient to support agriculture;
therefore, irrigation was practiced from early times and had its social
concomitant in the centralization of government within individual settlements and the development of systematized relations between settlements
to control the use of water. The north reached approximately its present
conformation in Pliocene times. The area dealt with here is an irregular
rocky plateau; the mountainous northern and eastern portions of the country have been too little explored archeologically to yield much information.
It possesses reasonably good building stone and some timber and has sufficient rainfall to permit agriculture without irrigation. Although its resources are such as to minimize the necessity of foreign trade, yet its lo-
cation along the top of the Fertile Crescent places it in the path of migra-
tory movements and commerce between Iran (and farther Asia) and the
lands bordering the Mediterranean. Hence at times the north shows contacts with Syria or Iran which are not found in the more isolated south.

This mention of differences between the two areas, however, should
not be construed as an implication of complete cultural separation between

them. North and south are usually allied culturally, showing greater similarity with each other than either has with any other land. The central part of the country—notably the Diyala region—often shows a transitional character; although more closely tied to the south, it may possess features of the northern culture unknown in the sites farther south. In discussing the problem of relative chronology in Mesopotamia, therefore, there are always two aspects: the relation of the archeological material from north and south and the relation of materials from either or both areas to those of other countries. Naturally, the foreign connections are chiefly with the bordering lands of Syria and Iran. The period covered begins with the food-producing stage, with village settlements, pottery, and domestic animals; it ends around 1500 B.C., when written records take pre-eminence in establishing chronology.

Mesopotamia has been relatively well explored archeologically, although more excavation in the northern and central parts of the country would be extremely helpful in elucidating the relations between north and south. And more knowledge of the historic period, particularly post-Early Dynastic, is badly needed.

The periods into which Mesopotamian materials are customarily divided are based in the prehistoric era on assemblages, usually with one dominant type of artifact, named for the site at which this artifact was first discovered. The system has obvious disadvantages, since the type-site never has all the components associated with the period by comparative study, and sometimes proves to be an aberrant representative of the culture—notably in the old "Jamdat Nasr" period, where the painted pottery first found at Jamdat Nasr proved to be by no means a universal element in the material culture of the latter part of the prehistoric age. However, where type-site names are given up, it is difficult to devise satisfactory substitutes. In the historic period political domination provides the names for the various phases: Early Dynastic, in which numerous small city-states held simultaneous sway; and then the successive hegemony of the dynasties of Akkad, Ur, etc. As will be seen, cultural differences correspond with the changes in political power.

The earliest demonstrable phase of village culture is the Hassuna period, remains of which are found only in the north in the Kirkuk and Mosul regions (Lloyd and Safar, 1945). Quite possibly southern Mesopotamia was still too marshy for settlement at that time. The Hassuna culture is on about the same general level as the Amuq phase A; and its standard pottery

wares, both painted and incised, show similarities with those of Amuq A-B
and the Proto-Chalcolithic of Mersin (Garstang, 1953, pp. 58-63). The
dark-burnished wares which are so abundant in the Syro-Cilician area are,
however, fairly rare in Mesopotamia and probably borrowed, if not imported, from the former. The same is true of the simple ground-stone
celts and a few rather well-made projectile points of chipped flint. Connection with Iran may be found in the clay sling missiles, which are common at Hassuna and known in Iran in Sialk I (Ghirshman, 1938, p. 24, Pl.
LII, 35). A further link with Iran is probably to be found in the Samarran
style of painted pottery (selected motifs on chart), which appears as a luxury ware contemporaneous with the standard Hassuna wares. It has been
suggested that Samarran is an outgrowth of the Hassunan painting style
(Leslie, 1952, pp. 57-66); but it seems more likely that the former is related to the pottery of the Buff Ware culture of Fars (particularly Giyan
V A-B), with which it shares various motifs (McCown, 1942a, p. 35).

The succeeding Halaf culture shows considerable advance, and, before the end of the phase, marked technical ability and no little artistry
are witnessed in the painted pottery which is its best-known product (selected motifs in Fig. 1) (Mallowan and Rose, 1935). Copper is known, although only a small amount has been found, and hard stone is worked into
vessels with no little skill. The best-developed and most consistent assemblages so far known come from the area around Mosul, with strong indication that the Halaf culture originated in that area, developing out of the
Hassuna stage with no notable outside influence. Halafian material is found
only in northern Mesopotamia, but village settlement in the south begins
during this era; for the earliest pottery from Eridu precedes the establishment of the Ubaid culture in the north and must be contemporaneous with
at least part of the Halaf culture (Lloyd and Safar, 1948). There are slight
resemblances between early Eridu pottery and Halaf pottery (it is difficult
to know how much because of the lack of adequate illustration of the Eridu
material); Eridu certainly does not belong to the Halaf culture, even peripheral Halaf; yet one gets the impression that the Eridu painters are not
completely ignorant of the Halaf style.

Halaf pottery is widely diffused (Perkins, 1949, pp. 43-45). Some has
been found at Tilki Tepe on Lake Van, and it is sometimes thought that the
Halaf culture originated there and spread into Mesopotamia from the northern mountains, but no material from the latter area which has yet been published substantiates this claim. Halaf pottery (both imported Mesopotamian

and local imitations) is found all through the western part of the Fertile Crescent: the Sinjar, the Khabur, the western Euphrates, Cilicia (Mersin XIX-XVII), and northern Syria clear to the Mediterranean coast (Amuq phase C, Ras Shamra IV, Hama L). In all cases it appears as something foreign added to local assemblages. There is no comparable diffusion to Iran, although Halafian motifs are found there at various dates. McCown has suggested reciprocal influence, with Halaf elements coming out of Mesopotamia around the end of the period and Iranian elements entering to form the basis of the succeeding Mesopotamian culture (McCown, 1942a, pp. 33-35; 1942b, pp. 427-29). This would presumably be connected with the general movements within Iran at the end of the Chashmah Ali phase, which shows a stage of culture comparable with Halaf in its technological improvements over the preceding phase: better-fired pottery, mud brick, use of hard stone, etc. (It is to be noted, however, that here and through-out the prehistoric period Iran is further advanced in metallurgy than Mesopotamia, and improvements visible in the latter country are probably due to contact with Iran.)

During the major part of the Halaf period, outside influences are lit-tle apparent in Mesopotamia. In the succeeding Ubaid age, however, this situation is markedly changed, for the distinctive elements of the Ubaid culture itself seem to have come from Iran at the end of the Chashmah Ali phase, around the time of Susa I, Bakun A, Sialk III, and Giyan V C (McCown, 1942a, Table II). Ubaid appears first in southern Mesopotamia, the earliest phase being so far known only at Eridu but probably present elsewhere also. In the north, Iranian influence begins at the end of the Halaf period (Gawra XX), with a marked increase, quite possibly connected with a movement of peoples, at the time of Gawra XIX. Painted pottery in a simpler and less adroit style than Halaf is characteristic, copper is somewhat more common, and at least in the latter part of the period there are rather complex settle-ments with monumental architecture (Perkins, 1949, pp. 46-96).

Northern and southern Mesopotamia can be tied together chronologi-cally with some assurance. The most important single factor is the fan-tastic "tortoise vase" (Fig. 1) appearing in the middle Ubaid phase of Eridu (levels XIII-VIII) and the early Ubaid of the north (Gawra XIX-XVII) (Lloyd and Safar, 1948, Pl. III; Tobler, 1950, Pl. CXXIII), and there are similar-ities in painted motifs from the same levels. The later phases in both areas have elements in common: the similarity of temple plans in Eridu XI-VI and Gawra XIII, the clay "bent nails" (Fig. 1) in Eridu XII-VI and

Gawra XIX-XII, and clay sickles (Fig. 1) in Eridu XII-VI and Ninevite 3 (Lloyd and Safar, 1948; Tobler, 1950; Mallowan, 1933).

Ubaid pottery, like Halaf, spreads to the Mediterranean; whether this is an outgrowth of migration, with Iranian settlers spreading all the way to Syria, or due to something like commercial contacts between Mesopotamia and the western lands is uncertain. The latter seems more likely, since there is no great disturbance of the older Syrian cultures and a transitional phase between Halaf and Ubaid (Amuq D) in Syria indicates a gradual introduction of the new elements.

After this period northern and southern Mesopotamia seem to go their own ways culturally, and in the age which for present purposes may be called "Late Prehistoric" (thereby avoiding the various controversial names for the local cultures), Mesopotamia shows two quite different cultures; but the two areas have some traits in common which can be used for dating purposes. The so-called "Uruk gray" and "Uruk red" wares (dark pottery, usually with a slipped and burnished surface and no other decoration), which represent a marked change from the earlier tradition of light-colored pottery with painted or incised decoration, are found in Warka XIV-III, Eridu "Early Uruk," Ninevite 3-4, Gawra XIa-VIII (Von Haller, 1932, pp. 37-41; Lloyd, 1948, pp. 44-47; Mallowan, 1933, pp. 163-166; Tobler, 1950, pp. 152, 154). Crudely made bowls of a coarse and heavy fabric, characteristically with sharply beveled rims (Fig. 1) are common in Warka XII-IV, Eridu "Late Uruk," Khafajah Protoliterate C, Nuzi IX-VIII, Ninevite 3-4, and Brak (Von Haller, 1932, Pl. 18, A; Lloyd, 1948, p. 49; Delougaz, 1952, p. 39; Starr, 1937-39, Pl. 50; Mallowan, 1933, p. 168; Mallowan, 1947, Pl. LXVI, 4). A squat bulging pot with medium neck and everted rim (Fig. 1) occurs in Khafajah Protoliterate C-D, Ninevite 4-5, and Gawra XIa-VII (Delougaz, 1952, p. 41, Pl. 187; Mallowan, 1933, Pl. LII; Tobler, 1950, Pl. CXLVII; Speiser, 1935, Pl. LXVI). Two sherds of a new type of painted pottery (Fig. 1), which begins in the north at the end of the period and is especially common in Ninevite 5, were found in the Diyala sites in Protoliterate and Early Dynastic contexts (Mallowan, 1933; Delougaz, 1952, Pls. 64, 16, and 133, i). The cylinder seal comes into use in the south, and several motifs of the style known as "Jamdat Nasr" (Fig. 1), which are ubiquitous in the southern sites, are found also in the north in Ninevite 4-5, Gawra VII, and the Brak Eye Temples (Frankfort, 1939; Mallowan, 1933, pp. 138-42; Speiser, 1935, Pl. LIX, 44, 46; Mallowan, 1947, Pl. XXI, 1-4). The pear-shaped macehead occurs in

Warka III, Gawra VIII, and the Brak Eye Temples (Nöldeke, 1936, Pl. 23, n-p; Speiser, 1935, Pl. XL, a; Mallowan, 1947, Pl. LII).

This is an age of considerable settlement, with new towns being founded all over the south. Such features as the tremendous and elaborate temple areas of Warka VI-III (Perkins, 1949, Figs. 16-17) and other sites are indications of wealth, religious complexity, and centralization of political power, with at least partial control over labor. The metals of the Gawra tombs of this age (Tobler, 1950, Pls. LVIII-LIX) show a fairly high stage of technology, although throughout the country copper tools and weapons are inferior to those of contemporaneous Iran and Syria. The most important invention of the age, writing, occurs only in the south.

Outside contacts are numerous. The gray and red burnished wares were certainly derived from some outside source. The former is often supposed to be Anatolian (Frankfort, 1932, pp. 30-40), but the "gray-ware people" of Hissar II should also be considered as a possible source and, since the latter site possesses various vessel forms which characterize the Ninevite 5 phase of Mesopotamia, seem somewhat more likely (Schmidt, 1937, pp. 112-14). The red ware may also have an Iranian origin, for red ware supplants Ubaid-like painted pottery in Bakun A V and Susa phase B, and the latter has also the beveled-rim bowls of Mesopotamia. Susa phase C and Sialk IV parallel the latter part of the Mesopotamian Late Prehistoric, possessing Proto-Elamite tablets, which show a comparable stage of writing, and cylinder seals of the Jamdat Nasr style; Sialk also has beveled-rim bowls and chalices of the Ninevite 5 type (for Iranian material see McCown, 1942a, pp. 43 f.; 1942b, pp. 439-44). There seems to have been somewhat less intimate contact with Syria; but Amuq G possesses Jamdat Nasr style seals, footed chalices like one from Gawra VII, and other Mesopotamian elements and is probably contemporaneous with the Ninevite 5 phase of the north, which continues into the early historic period. Amuq F must coincide with the earlier part of the Mesopotamian Late Prehistoric age.

The first historic age, the Early Dynastic period, is witnessed all over southern Mesopotamia as one of considerable technological progress, increasing urbanization, and noticeable wealth, culminating in the so-called "Royal Tombs" of Ur (Woolley, 1934). In the main, the culture is a development out of the prehistoric age. Written documents are numerous, especially in the latter part of the period, and the cuneiform script, used on clay tablets, is evolved. The period is practically nonexistent in the north, where the last phase of the prehistoric age connected with Ninevite 5 seems to continue until the time of Akkadian domination. Nor does the phase extend westward to any extent, although occasional cylinder seals, mostly of rather dubious Early Dynastic character, do appear in Syria and Palestine. But its influence is notable in the Elamite region of Iran, where Susa, Musyan, Khazineh, and Aliabad all show pottery, stone vessels, metals, cylinder seals, etc., of Mesopotamian Early Dynastic types (Gautier and Lampre, 1905; De Mecquenem, 1934). There is no particular outside influence in Mesopotamia.

The Akkadian period, the dynasty of Sargon of Akkad, shows a very different situation, being little known culturally in southern Mesopotamia save for the "Sargonid cemetery" (some of which is actually Early Dynastic) at Ur; but there is considerable written evidence for the Akkadian rulers and their exploits. In the north, cuneiform tablets now appear for the first time (Nuzi V-III, Brak Sargonid, Chagar Bazar II-III) (Starr, 1937-39, pp. 21-25; Mallowan, 1947, p. 66; Mallowan, 1937, p. 95), as well as occupation levels which provide some links with Ur and with the sequence in the Diyala region.

Gray burnished pottery characterizes the period in the north, and one of the most common forms is a well-made carinate bowl (Fig. 1) (e.g., Speiser, 1935, Pl. LXVII, 89); bowl and ware alike are probably developments of the gray ware of the Ninevite 5 phase, which is adequate explanation for their rarity in the south (the Diyala has a little gray ware and a few carinate bowls of somewhat similar type, but nothing very close). Bulging, wide-mouthed pots are also common in the north and relatively unknown in the south, although again the Diyala has a few in the Protoimperial-Akkadian range (e.g., Speiser, 1935, Pl. LXVIII; Delougaz, 1952, Pl. 162). "Teapots," rounded pots with tubular spouts (Fig. 1), are found in the Ur Sargonid cemetery, Diyala Akkadian levels, and Chagar Bazar II-III (Woolley, 1934, Pl. 265; Delougaz, 1952, Pl. 150; Mallowan, 1936, Fig. 15). Tall jars, ovoid or pear-shaped, usually with horizontally ribbed shoulders (Fig. 1), are known in Gawra VI, Brak Sargonid, Nuzi VI-V, and Diyala Protoimperial-Akkadian (Speiser, 1935, Pl. LXX, 143; Mallowan, 1947, Pl. LXVIII, 16; Starr, 1937-39, Pl. 53; Delougaz, 1952, Pl. 191). A prettily made lanceolate chipped-flint arrowhead (Fig. 1) is known in the Diyala Akkadian, Gawra VI, and Brak Sargonid (Speiser, 1935, Pl. XXXVIIIa, 18; Mallowan, 1947, Pl. XXXVII, 18-23).

It is noticeable that the metals generally associated with the late

Early Dynastic period (Ur Royal Cemetery) in the south occur only in Ak-
kadian context in the north. A pike-type, poker-butted spear and a cast
shaft-hole ax or adze (Fig. 1) are found in the Royal Cemetery, Gawra VI,
Billa V, and Brak Sargonid (Woolley, 1934, Pls. 223, 227; Speiser, 1935,
Pl. XLIX; Speiser, 1931, p. 21; Mallowan, 1947, Pl. XXXI, 11). Wide chisel
or ax blades, or molds for casting these, appear in the Royal Cemetery,
Gawra VI, Brak Sargonid, and Chagar Bazar II (Woolley, 1934, Pl. 229;
Speiser, 1935, Pl. XLVII; Mallowan, 1947, Pl. XXXI, 9; Mallowan, 1937,
Pl. XVIII B and Fig. 13, 1). The toggle-pin with simple head and upper
shank flattened for piercing (Fig. 1), which occurs in Gawra VI, Chagar
Bazar III, and Brak Sargonid, is related to pins in the Royal Cemetery of
Ur (Speiser, 1935, Pl. L, 8; Mallowan, 1937, Fig. 12, 5; Mallowan, 1947, Pl.
XXXI, 3-5; Woolley, 1934, Pl. 231). The hairpin with spatulate head (Fig. 1)
is known in the Royal Cemetery, Gawra VI, Billa V, and Brak Sargonid
(Woolley, 1934, Pl. 231; Speiser, 1935, Pl. L, 4; Speiser, 1932-33, p. 268;
Mallowan, 1947, Pl. LIII, 32). Lunate gold earrings are found in the Royal
Cemetery, Nuzi III, and Brak Sargonid (Woolley, 1934, Pl. 219; Starr,
1937-39, Pl. 55 I; Mallowan, 1947, Pl. XXXVI).

Connections with Syria are clear at this time; the Akkadian period
falls within the Amuq I-J range, probably toward the beginning, since this
range also contains material comparable to that of the succeeding Mesopotamian period. The I-J range has "teapots," little jars with relatively
wide mouths, toggle-pins, poker-butted spears, and molds for casting metal blades—all with Akkadian parallels. In Iran, Giyan IV has cast shaft-
hole axes, toggle-pins, and pike-spears (Contenau and Ghirshman, 1935,
Pl. 30); Hissar III has stone and metal vessels and various elaborate types
of jewelry connected with the Royal Cemetery of Ur and with the burned
city of Troy (Troy IIg) (Schmidt, 1937, pp. 208-17). By this time, Iran seems
to follow, rather than lead, Mesopotamia in the development of metal types
and definitely to have less close connections with Mesopotamia than in the
Early Dynastic period. In the case of all these international connections,
it is difficult to say which area is the borrower and which the lender; but,
in view of the political and economic power of the Akkadian dynasty, it is
likely that the common elements of material culture emanate from Mesopotamia.

The Gutian invasion put an end to Akkadian power in the south; in the
north destructions occur at the end of the Akkadian levels at Gawra, Brak,
Nuzi, and Assur and are probably also to be connected with the troubles at-

tendant on the Gutian invasion. The succeeding period saw the political domination of the south by the Third Dynasty of Ur, and probably a certain amount of control over the north also. There are a good many documents dating from this time, and much building was done at Ur, Warka, and other southern sites; unfortunately, little material other than architecture and written records has been published, and not much can be said about the general culture. The Diyala area offers little from this time, and northern Mesopotamia almost nothing. Assur Ishtar Temple E is dated by a tablet mentioning Bur-Sin of Ur, and Gawra V is tentatively equated with it on the basis of similarity of plan between its own shrine and the Ishtar Temple (Speiser, 1935, pp. 149 f.).

The next period of consequence culturally is the Larsa period, which is largely contemporaneous with the Old Babylonian and Old Assyrian periods. Northern and southern Mesopotamia do not share a common culture, and we are again handicapped by the relatively small amount of published artifactual material. The pottery from the Diyala sites forms the chief basis for comparisons, and it is particularly good for the late Larsa age. In the north the bulk of the material dates from the time of Chagar Bazar I, which begins in the reigns of Shamshi-Adad I of Assyria and Zimrilim of Mari. It is characterized by the type of painted pottery known as "Khabur ware," two typical examples of which are shown in Figure 1 (Mallowan, 1937, passim): round-bellied jars, with rounded shoulders and relatively narrow necks, and rather high bowls, with strongly marked rims. The painting is of the simplest: plain bands of dark paint or zones of very simple geometric design. Chagar Bazar I also has wide-mouthed pots (Fig. 1) of fine thin ware, which are paralleled in Old Babylonian levels in the Diyala region (Mallowan, 1936, Fig. 17, 4, 5; Delougaz, 1952, Pl. 161) and elsewhere, and fine cast axes (Fig. 1) (Mallowan, 1947, Pl. LV, 15).

Khabur ware is known in Syria also, although its dates are not certain. A simple type of painted pottery which has been called by that name occurs at Tell Atchana at a very early date; but until it is more fully published, one hesitates to equate it with the Mesopotamian Khabur ware of much more limited range of time. Somewhat similar painting occurs in Amuq I-J, and clear parallels to Khabur ware are to be found in Phases K-L. Until the evidence from all the western sites is available, we shall refrain from drawing exact chronological conclusions (see W. F. Albright, p. 32, above, and McCown, p. 65, below). It seems probable that the Khabur-type painted pottery came into Mesopotamia from Syria, where it seems rather more at home—or at least where local painting traditions are better established—but in Mesopotamia it was applied to local forms. Axes like those from Chagar Bazar I (Fig. 1) are known at Ras Shamra in contexts which must be seventeenth to sixteenth centuries by their similarities to Middle Bronze examples in Palestine (Schaeffer, 1948, Pl. X, with a different date). In Iran, Giyan II has bowls and simply decorated jars somewhat similar to Khabur ware, also projectile points with midrib and a cast ax similar to Chagar Bazar I specimens (Contenau and Ghirshman, 1935, Pls. 21-25). It is obvious that at this time there was a good deal of communication throughout western Asia; the connections of the Hammurabi dynasty of Babylon with Assyria, with Mari, and with western Syria (Atchana) are demonstrated by the correspondence; and the material remains bear this out. Further historical connections are known with Anatolia, for this is the period of the Kültepe tablets, when Assyrian merchants were settled in a colony in the Anatolian town.

The period ends with the spread of the white-on-black painted pottery variously called Nuzi ware, Atchana ware, Mitannian ware, etc., around 1500 B.C.

MESOPOTAMIA

	Tell Hassuna	Tell Arpachiyah	Eridu	Nineveh	Chagar Bazar	Tepe Gawra	Tell Brak	Tell Billa	Assur (Ishtar Temple)	Nuzi (L4 pit)	Diyah sites
Mitannian					III		Hurrian	III			
Old Babylonian / Old Assyrian / Larsa					I	IV / V	∿	IV	C / D	I-IIb	Old Babyl / Lar
Ur III							∿		E	∿	Gut / Ur I
Akkadian					II-III	VI	Sargonid	V	F / G	III-V / VI	Akkad
Early Dynastic				5	IV-V	VII-VIIIa	?	VI-VII	H	?	Prot imper / Ear Dyna I-III
Late Prehistoric			Temples I-V and "Uruk" levels	4	∿	VIIIb-XIa	Eye Temples			VII-IX	Prot. litera
Ubaid	XI-XII	1-5	Cemetery and Temples VI-XIII	3	∿	XII-XIX				X-XII	
Halaf	VI-X	6-10 and levels below	Temples XIV-XIX	2c	VI-XV	XX					
Hassuna	I-V			1-2b							

Figure 1

(WARKA ANNA)	FOREIGN RELATIONS	
	Amuq M Giyan I	
	Amuq K-L Giyan II Cappadocian colonies	
	Amuq I-J Hissar III Giyan IV	
I-II	Amuq G-H Susa C-D Hissar II	
I-XIV	Sialk IV	Cylinder seals
XV-XVIII - - -	Amuq D-E "Susa I" Bakun A Sialk III Giyan V c	
	Amuq C Chashmah Ali culture	
	Amuq A-B Giyan V A-B Sialk I	

53

References

Contenau, G., and R. Ghirshman. Fouilles du Tépé-Giyan près de Néhavend, 1931 et 1932. Paris: P. Geuthner, 1935.

Delougaz, Pinhas. Pottery from the Diyala Region. ("Oriental Institute Publications," Vol. LXIII.) Chicago: University of Chicago Press, 1952.

Frankfort, H. Archeology and the Sumerian Problem. ("Studies in Ancient Oriental Civilization," No. 4.) Chicago: University of Chicago Press, 1932.

_____. Cylinder Seals. London: Macmillan & Co., Ltd., 1939.

Garstang, John. Prehistoric Mersin. Oxford: Clarendon Press, 1953.

Gautier, J. E., and G. Lampre. Recherches archéologiques. ("Mémoires de la Délégation en Perse," Vol. VIII.) Paris: Ernest Leroux, Éditeur, 1905.

Ghirshman, Roman. Fouilles de Sialk près de Kashan, 1933, 1934, 1937. Paris: P. Geuthner, 1938.

Haller, A. von. In: A. Nöldeke et al., "Vierter vorläufiger Bericht über die von der Notgemeinschaft der deutschen Wissenschaften in Uruk," Abhandlungen der Preussischen Akademie der Wissenschaft, Phil.-hist. Kl. (1932), pp. 31-47.

Leslie, Charles. In: Braidwood, R. J., et al., "Mattarah," Journal of Near Eastern Studies, XI (1952), 2-75.

Lloyd, Seton. "Uruk Pottery," Sumer, IV (1948), 39-51.

Lloyd, Seton, and Safar, Fuad. "Tell Hassuna: Excavations by the Iraq Government Department of Antiquities," Journal of Near Eastern Studies, IV (1945), 255-89.

_____. "Eridu," Sumer, IV (1948), 115-25.

McCown, Donald E. The Comparative Stratigraphy of Early Iran. ("Studies in Ancient Oriental Civilization," No. 23.) Chicago: University of Chicago Press, 1942.

_____. "The Material Culture of Early Iran," Journal of Near Eastern Studies, I (1942), 424-49.

Mallowan, M. E. L. In: Thompson, R. Campbell, and Mallowan, M. E. L., "The British Museum Excavations at Nineveh, 1931-32," University of Liverpool, Annals of Archaeology and Anthropology, XX (1933), 71-186.

_____. "The Excavations at Tall Chagar Bazar and an Archaeological Survey of the Habur Region, 1934-35," Iraq, III (1936), 1-86.

_____. "The Excavations at Tall Chagar Bazar and an Archaeological Survey of the Habur Region. Second Campaign, 1936," ibid., IV (1937), 91-177.

_____. "Excavations at Brak and Chagar Bazar," ibid., IX (1947), 1-259.

Mallowan, M. E. L., and Rose, J. C. Prehistoric Assyria: Excavations at Tall Arpachiyah, 1933. London: Oxford University Press, 1935.

Mecquenem, R. de. In: Archéologie, métrologie, et numismatique susiennes. ("Mémoires de la Mission archéologique en Iran," Vol. XXV.) Paris: Librairie Ernest Leroux, 1934.

Nöldeke, A., et al. "Siebenter vorläufiger Bericht über die von der deutschen Forschungsgemeinschaft in Uruk-Warka unternommenen Ausgrabungen," Abhandlungen der Preussischen Akademie der Wissenschaft, Phil.-hist. Kl. (1936).

Perkins, Ann. The Comparative Archeology of Early Mesopotamia. ("Studies in Ancient Oriental Civilization," No. 25.) Chicago: University of Chicago Press, 1949.

Schaeffer, C. F. S. Stratigraphie comparée et chronologie de l'Asie Occidentale (IIIe et IIe millénaires). London: Geoffrey Cumberlege, Oxford University Press, 1948.

Schmidt, Erich F. Excavations at Tepe Hissar, Damghan. Philadelphia: University Museum, University of Pennsylvania, 1937.

Speiser, E. A. "Reports from Our Expeditions in Iraq," Bulletin of the American Schools of Oriental Research, No. 41 (1931), pp. 19-24.

_____. "The Pottery of Tell Billa," Museum Journal, University Museum, University of Pennsylvania, XXIII (1932-33), 249-83.

_____. Excavations at Tepe Gawra, Vol. I: Levels I-VIII. Philadelphia: University of Pennsylvania Press, 1935.

Starr, R. F. S. Nuzi. Cambridge, Mass.: Harvard University Press, 1937-39.

Tobler, A. J. Excavations at Tepe Gawra, Vol. II. Philadelphia: University of Pennsylvania Press, 1950.

Woolley, C. L. Ur Excavations, Vol. II: The Royal Cemetery. London: Oxford University Press, 1934.

The Relative Stratigraphy and Chronology of Iran

Donald E. McCown
Oriental Institute, University of Chicago

Ten years ago my study, The Comparative Stratigraphy of Early Iran, was published, and this will form the base for the earlier periods considered in this paper. Since then a limited amount of new archeological evidence has appeared and various criticisms have been made of the chronology in that study, besides which I wish to re-emphasize the limitations of the evidence available for use. In addition to this, the chronology of Baluchistan cultures down to the time of the Harappa civilization will be considered, as also that of Iranian sites down to the early part of the first millennium B.C.

Before proceeding with the subject of Iranian chronology, it is worth considering the method used. This involves three steps. The first is the correlation of the levels of Iranian sites with the same cultures, following which is a cross-correlation between different Iranian cultures. This results from establishing the time span of particular traits sufficiently individual so that their occurrence at different sites may be assumed with probability to denote contemporaneity. Yet in some cases diagnostic traits need not be contemporaneous. An example of such an exception is found in Giyan VC and D (McCown, 1942, pp. 18 f.) with the existence in both levels of traits typical of the Hissar culture. In such a case a dynamic explanation seems necessary here, that VC at Giyan is contemporaneous with the Hissar culture up to its end and that the Hissar elements in VD postdate the end of that culture and are due to its displacement.

The second step in the method followed is the correlation of cultures and their phases with the Mesopotamian sequence which provides the backbone for the chronology of areas peripheral to it. These two steps result, first, in the relative stratigraphy within Iran and then the absolute chronology of Iranian cultures by comparison with Mesopotamia after the middle of the third millenium. A third step is then desirable, a comparison of dated cultures in Iran and in other areas peripheral to Mesopotamia, such as Anatolia or the Indus Valley. This step should provide an additional check on the validity of the Iranian chronology; yet, with our present knowledge, my opinion is that it can do so only very approximately. The relative and absolute chronology in all these peripheral regions is still quite imprecise. It is not sufficiently exact so that, for example, when an Iranian culture and the Harappa civilization share characteristics suggesting contemporaneity and yet correlate with different Mesopotamian periods, we can say more than that one of the two may be incorrectly dated or the disparity may be due to some factor now unknown. Consequently, I believe this third step cannot have great weight at present for checking Mesopotamian comparisons, which are the primary source for dating cultures peripheral to Iraq.

Now to the earliest Iranian cultures. Iran before the Warka period was divided into two main culture areas, one in the west and south with a Buff Ware culture, divided into regional aspects with somewhat varying phases of development, and the other in the north-center and north-east, with three successive cultures named after Sialk, Chashmah Ali, and Hissar. All these were simple village cultures, with a pastoral and agricultural life but with an increasing inventory of equipment as time passed.

In the latter area it should be noted that the stage represented at Jarmo in Iraq is still unknown. New evidence is slight. When Professor Carl Coon publishes his results from caves in Mazanderan, my theory (ibid., p. 2) that the red ware of Sialk I was an individual fabric distinct from the buff-colored ware of that level and connected with the red ware of Sialk II will, I believe, be confirmed. I have also seen pottery of the Chashmah Ali culture in the shop of an antiquities dealer in Teheran said to come from Azerbaijan. Since there was no reason to doubt the veracity of the ascription, it is likely that this culture existed in all the most northern part of Iran.

In the area of the Buff Ware culture we can now see that the remains of Bakun BI correspond to the cultural stage of Jarmo, though there is no evidence to prove that the level is that old.

The publication of results from three sites in the Susa area, Jafferabad, Jowi, and Bendebal (Le Breton, 1947), is a most significant source of new material. Only a limited selection of the finds is published. There is no proper stratification by floor levels, nor was architecture recovered. Objects were recorded by depth and are adequately described, though there is no quantitative analysis of pottery designs and forms, a prerequisite to sure relative stratigraphy. Nevertheless, we can now recognize successive aspects of the Buff Ware culture in Khuzistan. The sequence, which must be defined in terms of sites and depth-levels, seems with moderate certainty to be as follows: (1) Jafferabad, 3.5-6 meters, the Jafferabad aspect; (2) Jafferabad, 2-3.5 meters, Jowi; Bendebal, 2-6 meters, the Jowi aspect; (3) Bendebal, 0-2 meters, Buhallan, the Bendebal aspect; (4) Jafferabad, 0-2 meters, Susa I, the Susa I aspect. The first of these stages may be contemporaneous with Giyan VA. As at Giyan, there is a considerable difference between the pottery of this and the succeeding phases. The Jowi and Bendebal aspects are characterized by the development of the same design style. They are likely to be contemporary with Bakun BII through Bakun AIV and to Giyan VB and C up to 13 - 14 meters. There may be a gap between stages 3 and 4, in which could occur a formative stage of the Susa I style, for the last phase is that of the well-known Susa I pottery found with orange-red ware of Uruk type and that known from Bakun AV.

There is no new evidence to suggest a change in my correlation of the Buff Ware aspects with the northern cultures or with those in Mesopotamia. I should like, however, to point out how tenuous the evidence is. The traits on which correlations depend are known only from publications giving a selection of materials without a quantitative analysis of them. As a result, the precise time range of such traits is clearly uncertain, as well as what is truly typical of each level. This is true of the materials from all sites excavated except for Bakun A and later tomb groups from sites like Giyan and Sialk. Furthermore, the correlation of all Buff Ware aspects with the northern cultures depends primarily on signs of direct contact between Giyan V and the Chashmah Ali and Hissar cultures. For a surer correlation of the Buff Ware and northern cultures we need an excavated site in the region west of Isfahan, for example, where the two culture areas should have met. In Fars the stratigraphy is very weak. A site is needed to fill the gap between Bakun B and A, for Level II of the former is not proved stratigraphically earlier than the latter. Finally, during all periods covered by this paper the stratified sites are few and separated by very considerable distances. Excavations at a site like Der, near Badrah in Iraq, or others on either side of the Iraq-Iran border are required to fix the absolute chronology of western Iran. The results presently attainable are thus clearly far from conclusive but are the most likely with the information available.

In connection with Mesopotamian relationships, the new Susa area sequence has a bearing on the earliest materials from Eridu in southern Iraq.

Early Eridu vessel forms (Lloyd and Safar, 1948, Pl. III, 25-32) are in
the range of the Jowi aspect. The designs of the same level (ibid., Pl. X)
are similar to those of the Jafferabad and Jowi aspects. I would specu-
late that the earliest Eridu pottery represents an extension of the Jafferabad and Jowi aspects into southern Iraq. This stage at Eridu is thus pre-
Ubaid in time as well as culturally, in·the sense that it is not directly an-
central to the Ubaid culture. The early Eridu material is thus Iranian, as
is the Ubaid culture, the former representing a limited settlement of Ira-
nians, the latter a much more widespread migration. Early Eridu may
thus best be called "Ubaid-precursor."

For the time of the Warka and Protoliterate periods there is some
new evidence from Khuzistan, the only area in western Iran where there
is no gap at the stratified sites following the end of the Buff Ware culture.
As already mentioned, Susa I is now known to correspond to an early part
of the Warka period. The best evidence for this time will be published
when the opportunity arrives to work up materials from my excavations
at Tall-i-Ghazir, a site almost due east of Ahwaz and not far north of Ram
Hormuz. Here the lowest levels contained Buff Ware pottery, poorly stratified, since the trench found it at the edge of the settlement. Above it were
twenty-four floors to a depth of 11.5 meters, corresponding to the Warka
and earlier Protoliterate periods and Susa B. All I can say at present is
that the pottery in these levels shows great similarity to, as well as considerable differences from, that in Iraq. As an example of the divergences,
reserved slip ware occurs in the middle of this sequence and not at all in
what should be Protoliterate levels. The topmost prehistoric layer was
1.5 meters thick, with two floors. It is late Protoliterate, containing Jamdat Nasr type objects, a proto-Elamite tablet, and painted pottery which is
essentially Jamdat Nasr in style, though not with a true plum-colored slip.
As at Susa, the level equated with the Warka and Protoliterate periods is
very substantial. This is additional confirmation that the end of the Buff
Ware culture and, by inference, of the Hissar culture must be separated
by a fair amount of time from Giyan IV and Sialk IV, for example. It is
consequently not likely, as some French archeologists have insisted, that
the Buff Ware and Hissar cultures continued so long into the time of the
Warka and even Protoliterate periods that there was no, or at best a very
short, interval between them and the cultures which followed. It is pertinent at this place to consider one point arising from the radioactive carbon dating of Jarmo, now practically certain around 4700 B.C. This date

signifies that all the later prehistoric sequence down to the Early Dynastic period must be considerably shorter than was believed ten years ago and that the various periods followed each other more rapidly than was suspected, though they were not, of course, of equal length. What is needed for all the prehistoric periods is a sequence of such dates.

In the earlier third millennium at Susa the style of Susa II does not continue beyond the Akkadian period at the latest, as shown by De Mecquenem's publication of graves (De Mecquenem, 1943, pp. 76-126). The culture of Giyan IV in the Zagros north of Susa seems to have the same time range as Susa D. It is now known also to occur, perhaps in a late stage, in Fars, where it has been discovered at Tall-i-Chagal, Gashak, not far south of Persepolis, in soundings of the Iranian Antiquities Service.

In northeastern Iran we must still depend on the sequence of Hissar II and III, despite the final publication of the excavations at Shah Tepe. At both sites most of the material is from graves, but at Hissar a good deal of material from Levels IIB and IIIB and C was found in house strata, giving a surer stratification than is possible from a grave sequence.

The Shah Tepe publication (Arne, 1945) is an excellent report of the objects discovered, but the level designations used do not correspond to archeological strata. They refer to groups of tombs at particular depths in the mound. As a result, these "levels" contain a mixture of what are actually successive object types. To be distinguished are four groups of pottery types, the pottery of each group consistently associated within that group. These should be successive and date from the time of Hissar IIB through IIIC.

Despite the problem of determining the grave sequence at Shah Tepe, there is a clear difference in ceramic sequence there and at Hissar. If it is correct to consider the cultures at the two sites the same, they are far from uniform in their pottery. Also interesting is the reappearance of footed vessels in the topmost levels of the site, which suggests the reintroduction of a Hissar II type element. To be noted further is the absence of ceramic features of Hissar I type in the pottery of Shah Tepe III.

The culture of Anau III, as represented by distinctive incised pottery, is now known within the limits of Iran. It was discovered at a disturbed site near Nishapur by the Metropolitan Museum expedition. The prospect is, therefore, good of finding a site with Hissar III and Anau III materials which will permit the precise correlation of these two cultures.

Some controversy has arisen over my dating of the end of Hissar III.

Piggott (1943, pp. 169 ff.) has argued, on the basis of Baluchistan and Indus Valley evidence, that the last culture at Hissar must have continued
into the second millennium. As remarked earlier, Hissar III can be dated
securely in relation to Mesopotamia only. Indian evidence can "date" no
sequence in Iran; it can merely raise a question as to the validity of dating there or indicate that we know too little to explain signs of Iranian and
Indian contacts. As will be seen later, the Baluchistan sequence and the
date of the Harappa civilization are too uncertain to use in checking Iranian chronology.

At the same time, I wish to point out the real uncertainties in the dating of Hissar III. In large part, this dating depends on a fairly large number of elements found at Hissar and in Iraq not later than the Akkadian period. The first uncertainty is due to insufficient knowledge of materials
from the Third Dynasty of Ur and the Old Babylonian period. As a result,
elements used in dating Hissar III might have had a longer life in Mesopotamia than we now know. The second uncertainty is due to the possibility
that Sumerian styles and types of objects, once taken over in peripheral
areas, may have had a longer life there than in Sumer. Because of this
situation, I feel that the best evidence, though quantitatively slight, is provided by comparisons between Hissar III, Giyan IV, and Susa D (McCown,
1942, Fig. 16). Particularly important is a spear with bent tang-tip found
in all three levels. This is a non-Mesopotamian form characteristic in
Iran only of Hissar III. Susa D, clearly, and Giyan IV, with considerable
probability, are not later than the Akkadian period, according to Mesopotamian evidence, proving the existence of this form of spear in Iran around
the middle of the third millennium (contrary to the statement in Maxwell-
Hyslop, 1946, pp. 29, 32). It seems most logical to assume that these implements reached Susa and Giyan from the culture of Hissar III rather than
to postulate that they must have come from Syria or the Aegean area,
where the type is well known several hundred years later. In other words,
Hissar III must be dated by Iranian and Mesopotamian evidence rather
than by that from sites far to the west (cf. Foreword, p. ix, and Goldman,
p. 75 below). Some day the excavation of a mound in northeastern Iran
will determine what culture followed Hissar III and thus finally settle the
problem.

Similar is the case with Indus Valley comparisons. Objects from
Hissar III are identical with some from Indus sites, where they appear
at the end of, and immediately following, the Harappa civilization. There

is no factual evidence for dating the end of that civilization, now connected with considerable probability with the arrival of the Aryans in India. This event is assumed to fall in the second quarter of the second millennium on the basis of the time required for the transmission of the Rig-Veda. On such grounds it is obviously precarious to reduce the date of the Hissar III culture to the first half of the second millennium. Actually, the only date known for the Harappa civilization is that some part of its classical phase falls during the Akkadian period. At present it is possible to do no more than guess when it began and ended. I would add in this connection that it is well to remember that Krogman considered the racial types of Hissar III to include Nordics.

Before continuing with later Iranian sites, we will turn to the cultures of Baluchistan and the Indus Valley. Publication of the results of the Fairservis expedition (Fairservis, 1952), from around Quetta, the Zhob-Loralai area, and Afghanistan, should give a precision to the relative chronology of the cultures of this region which does not exist with the evidence now available. Since no trustworthy stratigraphy exists for Baluchistan, all that is possible at present is a definition of ceramic types and an indication of their succession on the basis of extremely limited evidence.

In southern Baluchistan the earliest ceramic is Niain ware, known from excavations by Sir Aurel Stein at Niain Buthi in Las Bela. This material I have analyzed for a forthcoming memoir of the Archaeological Survey of India detailing Sir Aurel's final explorations. It is a red ware with plum or brown slips on bowls or goblets with designs in black paint. At the type site it is proved stratigraphically older than Nal and Kulli wares, and, as it is found over all of southern Baluchistan excepting the Kej Valley, this is probably true for the whole area. Recently this has been called "Togau ware" (De Cardi, 1950, Pl. I, 4-9). I believe the term "Niain ware" is preferable, since its excavation and stratification at Niain Buthi considerably antedate its later recognition.

Next comes the Nal culture, as indicated by its appearance in stratified Indus sites (Deva and McCown, 1949, pp. 24 f.). It seems to end at the beginning of the Harappa civilization and to be contemporary with the Amri culture. Two stages are typologically distinguishable, typified by Siah-damb, Nundarah, and Sohr-damb, Nal.

The Kulli culture follows, beginning at the commencement of the Harappa civilization, again on Indus Valley evidence (ibid., p. 25 and n. 5).

My study of all the materials from the sites of Kulli and Mehi in the Central Asian Antiquities Museum, the gross stratigraphy at the former site, and the appearance of certain designs in preclassical Harappan remains at Pandi Wahi and Ghazi Shah have allowed the recognition of two phases of this culture, the earlier represented by the Kulli site and the later at Mehi.

Little can be said of Quetta ware, which should be placed chronologically by the results of the Fairservis expedition. Stylistically, it is closer to the buff ware of Iran than any of its other eastern offshoots. Nevertheless, it is doubtless later than its Iranian parent, as indicated by its ware and shapes, as well as by still earlier ceramics found by Fairservis.

To the pre-Harappan Amri ware of the Indus may now be added another discovered by Stein at Kalepar in Bahawalpur. This, too, is pre-Harappan, and its design shows some similarities to Amri and Quetta pottery, though it is a separate ware.

Now as to relationships and dating. Amri is pre-Harappan and thus likely to be Early Dynastic and possibly earlier. Nal, Kalepar, and at least part of the Quetta ware are roughly contemporary. Niain is earlier and thus likely to be at least Protoliterate in date. The Kulli culture is contemporary with the Harappa civilization and thus late Early Dynastic through Akkadian and possibly later. Niain ware cannot be related surely to any other. The Nal, Quetta, Amri, and Kalepar wares are splinter groups from the older Buff Ware culture of Iran. Kulli contains some elements of Buff Ware design, which may derive from Nal and perhaps Quetta; but it is not a Buff Ware offshoot, and I would guess that it might be related to one of the elements original to the Harappa civilization.

In southwestern Baluchistan another ware is known from burials at Shahi Tump (Stein, 1931, pp. 93-103) and is further found in the Rakhshan, Seistan, and Bampur areas. A comparison of the stratified pottery from Bampur and tombs at Khurab (Stein, 1937, pp. 106-12, 118-25) suggests that the latter date late in the Bampur culture. It is at Khurab that the greatest similarities to the Shahi Tump tomb material occur. Furthermore, certain vessels from Khurab (ibid., Pls. XXXII, 9; XXXIII, 15) compare very closely with examples from a burial toward the end of the Mehi stage of the Kulli culture (Stein, 1931, Pl. XXX, Mehi III, vi, 2, 13). Thus the end of the Bampur culture and the Shahi Tump ware would date around the end of the Kulli culture. The beginning of the Bampur culture extends back into the time of Early Dynastic Mesopotamia, as shown by distinctively carved stone vessels common to both.

In Seistan an aggregation of pottery is known from wind-eroded sites. Alongside ceramic types distinctive of Seistan are Bampur and Shahi Tump wares. The Seistan pottery probably dates as they do. Its chronology will become more precise as this pottery is discovered in stratified sites in the Quetta area and southern Afghanistan.

In northern Baluchistan there is a separate ceramic type in the Pishin area. This is red pottery with red and black painted designs (Stein, 1929, Pl. XXI, Sp. H.1, Ks. 4, Sp. M.6, on none of which does the red paint show distinctly in the photographs). It is undated at present, though some early Kulli patterns are found at Pishin sites.

In the Zhob-Loralai area the stratigraphy depends on the Ross collection from Rana Ghundai (Ross, 1946). As a result, the ceramic sequence of this region depends on (1) a handful of stratified sherds and (2) the stylistic equivalence of pottery from surface collections at other sites with the few stratified examples from Rana Ghundai. The sequence is very likely to extend from at least the time of the late Protoliterate through the Harappa civilization. A hint is given by one unpublished sherd that Rana Ghundai B may be as late as the Kulli phase of the Kulli culture, though it could also overlap with Nal. Rana Ghundai A and B show marked similarities to the Hissar culture. These disappear in the C and D pottery from this site. I suspect a parallelism here with the change between the Buff Ware-derived Nal pottery and the succeeding Kulli culture ware, and I suggest that the disappearance of Iranian-derived elements in the Kulli culture and in Rana Ghundai C-D, as also the disappearance of the Amri culture, occurs at about the same time and is related to events, not discernible at present, connected with the beginning of the Harappa civilization.

The short space that remains will be devoted to the later remains in Iran. From the latter part of the third millennium down to the Achaemenian period, woefully little is known of Iranian cultures. There are only two stratified sites for all this time, Tepe Giyan and Susa. At Susa we can recognize Mesopotamian-type artifacts for the Ur III, Kassite, Assyrian, and Neo-Babylonian periods; but purely Iranian elements are hidden, in the main, by inadequate reporting of what was found.

At Giyan the sequence is essentially one of tombs. Giyan III supplants the culture of Giyan IV and is known into south-central Luristan. It appears again at Tall-i-Chagal, Gashak, near Persepolis, showing how much

more widespread this culture must have been than has been known. It
dates from not later than Ur III (McCown, 1942, p. 48 and n. 90) to the First
Dynasty of Babylon (seal in Tomb 3 at Jamshedi).

At Tepe Giyan there appears to be a gap in the tomb sequence between
Giyan III and II. This, I believe, is indicated by tombs at Bad Hora, in
which there is a mixture of ceramic traits of both II and III, suggesting that
the Bad Hora tombs are transitional between the two cultures. On this evidence the beginning of the culture of Giyan II follows immediately the end
of Giyan III about the time of the First Dynasty of Babylon. Its end is dated
to the fourteenth century by a Nuzi-type seal in Tomb 68 and another outside the tombs (Contenau and Ghirshman, 1935, Pl. 38, 4) at a level from
which the latest II tombs should have been sunk. Obviously, a cylinder
seal loose in the dirt is undependable evidence, and the end of this period
could well be somewhat later. Similarities to Khabur ware, which dies out
in Mesopotamia during the First Dynasty of Babylon, occur in the pottery
of this level. Either Giyan II should begin earlier than present evidence
suggests, or the end of the Khabur ware saw its penetration into and continuation in Iran (cf. Albright, p. 32, and Perkins, p. 50 above).

The succeeding period, Giyan I, shows a transition from II. Its end
is dated by architecture close to the top of the mound to about the eighth
century (Ghirshman, 1939, p. 95).

This is the approximate sequence known for northern Luristan—approximate, since one hundred-odd tombs covering over a thousand years
can hardly be expected to represent adequately the cultures involved.

In north-central Iran two cemeteries at Sialk, dating either side of
1000 B.C., furnish the first evidence for the cultures of this part of the
country since the time of the Protoliterate period. Ghirshman's dates
for Sialk V and VI (ibid., respectively, pp. 21 and 95) seem as accurate as
is presently possible. It is worth noting that the duration of each cemetery can be only guessed at. Sialk V could date earlier than Ghirshman
believes, since the iron found in one grave dates only that grave and not
the whole cemetery, part of which could be pre-Iron Age.

A word should be devoted to the Luristan bronzes, by which I mean
the decorated bronzes. To consider the various arguments for their dating is pointless, since the publication of the excavations of the Holmes
Luristan Expedition will show a large class of them to be late Assyrian.

I have left to the last the stratification of Geoy Tepe in Azerbaijan
(Burton Brown, 1951). It is a most difficult site to deal with, since in

many respects it is less Iranian in character than Caucasian or Anatolian. Eight levels were distinguished. The fifth, Level D, contained iron and thus should date from the latter half of the second millennium onward, and probably late rather than early in this time range. The later levels are consequently all Iron Age and could extend practically to the Median period. Some of the pottery, particularly from Levels C and D, shows a general resemblance to Vannic ware, but no identity (Osten, 1952). There are two substantial earlier levels, K and M. At the top of K a raquet pin was discovered which suggests a terminal date not later than the Akkadian period (Mallowan, 1947, p. 213, no. 32). If this is true, a gap of a millennium must separate Levels K and D. This is not unlikely, since materials found not far to the south at Dinkha and Gird-i-Hassan Ali (McCown, 1942, pp. 49 f.) are not represented at Geoy Tepe, suggesting that the sequence there is incomplete. As to the painted pottery of Level M, it is not Buff Ware, and no good parallels to it exist. I see no means of dating it at present.

Finally, this paper should have made clear that most of our conclusions are in the nature of hypotheses. Many are likely to prove correct, but their greatest immediate value is to point out problems requiring further investigation in future excavations. We know less about Iran than there remains to be learned about its known and still undiscovered cultures.

Table 1

MESOPOTAMIA	GEOY	ANAU	SHAH	TU-RANG	CHASH-MAH ALI	HISSAR	SIALK	GIYAN	SUSA	SUSA AS-PECT	BAKUN	INDUS	S. BALU-CHI-STAN	SHAHI TUMP	RANA GHUN-DAI
ASSYRIA 1000-	A														
KASSITE 1500-	D / G						VI / V								
OLD BABY-LONIAN 2000-															
UR III 2100-												JU-KHAR			D
AKKADIAN 2300-	K →														C
EARLY DYNASTIC		III	II	106 m.		III		IV	D		A V / A IV	HA-RAPPA	KULLI		B
PROTO-LITERATE		II	III	97 m.		II	IV	III	C		A I / B II	AMRI KALE-PAR	NAL NIAIN	SEI-STAN BAM-PUR	A
WARKA		I			I B	I	III	V D / V C	B / I	BU-HAL-LAN	A V / A IV				
UBAID					I A		II	V C			A I				
HALAF							I	V B		JOWI JAF-FER-ABAD	B II				
SAMARRA								V A			B I				
HASSUNA															
JARMO 4700															

References

Arne, T. J. Excavations at Shah Tepe, Iran. ("Reports from the Scientific Expedition to the Northwestern Provinces of China under the Leadership of Dr. Sven Hedin," Vol. VII, Part 5.) Stockholm: Sino-Swedish Expedition, 1945.

Burton Brown, T. Excavations in Azerbaijan, 1948. London: Murray, 1951.

Cardi, B. de. "On the Borders of Pakistan: Recent Explorations," Arts and Letters: Journal of the Royal India, Pakistan, and Ceylon Society, XXIV (1950), 252-57.

Contenau, G., and Ghirshman, R. Fouilles du Tépé-Giyan, près de Néhevand, 1931 et 1932. Paris: Geuthner, 1935.

Deva, K., and McCown, D. E. "Further Explorations in Sind: 1938," Ancient India, No. 5 (1949), pp. 12-30.

Fairservis, W. A., Jr. "Preliminary Report on the Prehistoric Archaeology of the Afghan-Baluchi Areas," Novitates, American Museum of Natural History, No. 1587 (1952), pp. 1-39.

Ghirshman, R. Fouilles de Sialk près de Kashan 1933, 1934, 1937, Vol. II. Paris: Geuthner, 1939.

Le Breton, L. Note sur la céramique peinte aux environs de Suse et à Suse, pp. 120-219. ("Mémoires de la Mission archéologique en Iran," Vol. XXX [1947].)

Lloyd, S., and Safar, F. "Eridu," Sumer, IV, No. 2 (1948), 115-27.

McCown, D. E. The Comparative Stratigraphy of Early Iran. Chicago: University of Chicago Press, 1942.

Mallowan, M. E. L. "Excavations at Brak and Chagar Bazar," Iraq, IX (1947), 1-259.

Maxwell-Hyslop, R. "Daggers and Swords in Western Asia," Iraq, VIII (1946), 1-65.

Mecquenem, R. de. Fouilles de Suse, 1933-1939, pp. 3-161. ("Mémoires de la Mission archéologique en Iran," Vol. XXIX.)

Osten, H. H. von der. "Die urartäische Töpferei aus Van und der Möglichkeiten ihrer Einordnung in die anatolische Keramik," Orientalia, N.S., XXI (1952), 307-28.

Piggott, S. "Dating the Hissar Sequence—the Indian Evidence," Antiquity, XVII (1943), 169-82.

Ross, Brigadier E. J. "A Chalcolithic Site in Northern Baluchistan," Journal of Near Eastern Studies, V (1946), 284-316.

Stein, Sir M. A. An Archaeological Tour in Waziristān and Northern Balūchistān. ("Memoirs of the Archaeological Survey of India," No. 37.) 1929.

_____. An Archaeological Tour in Gedrosia. ("Memoirs of the Archaeological Survey of India," No. 43.) 1931.

_____. Archaeological Reconnaissances in North-western India and South-eastern Iran. London: Macmillan & Co., Ltd., 1937.

The Relative Chronology of Southeastern Anatolia

Hetty Goldman
Institute for Advanced Study, Princeton, New Jersey

The position of Cilicia on the main road which leads from central Anatolia to northern Syria makes it an important link in the archeology of these two regions. The preponderance of influence emanating either from Anatolia or from Syria changes markedly under different historical pressures and at different periods. The evidence is drawn chiefly from the sites of Mersin (Garstang, 1937, 1938, 1953) and Tarsus (Goldman, 1935, 1937, 1938, 1940), so close together that they are practically identical in culture. They will not be treated separately except in the very few instances where the evidence does not seem to agree. Unfortunately, these are the only two sites that have been sufficiently examined to produce reliable results. An excavation along the Pyramos River (Ceyhan) penetrating to the Neolithic and Bronze Age levels is urgently needed. The whole of prehistoric southwestern Anatolia remains terra incognita except for the surface examination of mounds around Antal,ʲa (Ormerod, 1909-13). Only such ceramic wares in the Cilician repertoire as are paralleled elsewhere will be mentioned.

Neolithic

At neither Mersin nor Tarsus could the full depth of the Neolithic deposit be reached, but Professor Garstang at Mersin carried the excavation through 9 meters (Garstang, 1953, p. 11), so that the general character can hardly be in doubt. While the dark-faced Neolithic pottery resembles that of the whole region, which runs on a line approximately due east to the Kurdish highlands (Perkins, 1949, p. 15) beyond Mosul, it must be emphasized that for the present the closer relationships have a much narrower range. Sakje Geuzi, for example, while showing some striking resemblances with Cilicia in the black polished pottery with bands of pricked design (Garstang, Phythian-Adams, and Seton-Williams, 1937, Pl. XXV, 9-10, 16), and possibly in patterns such as the bands of very fine shallow diagonal crosshatching (ibid., Pl. XXIII, 1, 3), has other designs and, above all, shapes not paralleled at Cilicia. The direct links of Cilicia are with northern Syria and Palestine, especially with Ras Shamra V, Hama M, Amuq A-C, Jericho X-XVII. The light crumbly wares of Cilician Neolithic are also present at Amuq in Phases A and B. To this general picture must now be added the extraordinary revelations which include fortification walls and well-built houses in the present excavations at Jericho (Kenyon, 1952, p. 73). It does not seem too bold to prophesy that in Cilicia, too, similar, if not equally brilliant, phases of this culture may be found; for it is adumbrated by the well-laid stone walls of Mersin (Garstang, 1953, Pls. IIa, IV, a-c) and numerous fragments of highly polished wall plaster which have turned up sporadically at both Tarsus and Mersin, as well as rather inconclusive evidence for a level of stone pottery preceding the ceramic phase (Garstang, 1953, pp. 16 ff.).

Chalcolithic

The Chalcolithic of Cilicia is closely tied to that of northern Syria and Mesopotamia, for the successive phases of Hassuna, Tell Halaf, Ubaid, and Uruk are all present, although in a provincial and weakened form. This holds for all but the gray Uruk, which is of fine quality. The question of the origin of this gray ware cannot be discussed here, but it is well to remember that Anatolia and regions far to the east and north, such as Anau (Pumpelly, 1908, pp. 132 ff.) across the Caspian and northern Iran (McCown, 1942, p. 12), are the home of gray monochrome ware. In the last phase of the Chalcolithic period the evidence of Tarsus, scant as it is, indicates a preponderance of chevron-painted ware, derived ultimately from Halafian motifs, which is not paralleled at Mersin. Jemdet Nasr ware is not represented, but certain unstratified seals from Tarsus are closely linked with this period. With the end of the Chalcolithic period, we come to a second discrepancy between Tarsus and Mersin, in that the white-painted black ware of Mersin was not found at Tarsus. Professor Garstang has offered a plausible explanation (Garstang, 1953, pp. 185 ff.); but a closer examination of the Tarsus stratigraphy suggests the possibility that this transitional period between Chalcolithic and Early Bronze may be missing, not so much on the site as a whole as in the area excavated. A few fragments of the characteristic pedestals were found at Tarsus, though in lighter wares, but nothing more; and, as the excavations were carried on within the narrower limits of a pit (ca. 10.50 x 7.00 meters) in a region which apparently lay outside the village and contained much village refuse, a larger area, more advantageously placed, might still disclose some ware of this type.

Early Bronze I

Early Bronze I was a long transitional period, with a depth at Tarsus of about 8 meters. Its beginnings, however, were clearly marked by the first introduction of the red gritty or sandy wares so characteristic of all the three periods of Early Bronze; and linked to it was the characteristic Anatolian shape of pitcher with rising spout. This red ware can be equated with Qal'at er-Rus stone ware of Level XIII (Ehrich, A., 1939, pp. 27 ff.). In Cilicia the fabric of the red ware shows great variety. It may be exceedingly impure, with many lime and other stone inclusions, or it may be well levigated, sandy, and a pure brick-red or rosy pink. When thin and hard fired—and it is for the most part well fired—it is clinky and may turn brown or gray. The finer ware is probably related to the brittle orange ware of Amuq H. It was the utility ware all through the Early Bronze Age and was used both for very large shapes, such as pitchers, and for smaller household dishes. In order to lighten the vessel, the walls were thinned either by finger-streaking the inner surface or by finger-pressing the walls. Outside the Syrian parallels already quoted, no others have as yet been found; and in Cilicia it may well be a ware introduced suddenly from outside, possibly from Syria, but developed with great variety of shape and fabric within Cilicia itself.

Variants of red gritty ware are: (a) comb-impressed ware, found at Qal'at er-Rus, Level XII-V (Ehrich, A., 1939, p. 30); (b) scored ware, which is, I believe, similar to the scored ware which makes its appearance in Troy Id (Blegen, Caskey, Rawson, and Sperling, 1950, pp. 39, 53), although it is there attributed to the Aegean, for it is described as a red ware apparently very similar to, though not identical with, the Cilician fabric.

The Early Bronze I period was one of transition, when a great deal of the typical chaff-faced Chalcolithic fabric was still in use. Although painting was continued, it was reduced to simple parallel or vertical bands. Viewed as a whole, Early Bronze I might be described as a period in which the affiliations with northern Syria and Mesopotamia were weakening and those with Anatolia had not yet been strongly established.

Early Bronze II[1]

Early Bronze II shows a certain very distinctive local character but

---

1. An illustration of a red polished incised pitcher of Early Bronze II period has been included in the illustrations (Fig. 1, a_1), in order to enable Mr. Ehrich in his paper on "The Relative Chronology of South-

is nevertheless more firmly linked with other regions.

The red gritty ware is now decorated with a variety of incised ornament, each variant having its own typical shapes. It was the basic material for a type of shallow incision (cross-stitch incision), which has its
parallels in Syria at Sinjirli (Von Luschan, pp. 38 f., Pls. 15 and 16, a-d)
and Amuq H (brittle orange ware).

The black incised wares, which had already reached a developed stage
in Early Bronze I, now show great variety of decoration but are not closely linked in pattern or shape with those of central and northwestern Anatolia, as far as we know the material. The type of incision and some of
the patterns show striking resemblances to the Syrian wares of Amuq H,
where, however, they are apparently found almost exclusively on lids.
The bowl and cup shapes of Cilicia and the use of rather elaborate dis-
jointed patterns (Fig. 1, a) point rather to Cyprus (Schaeffer, 1936, Fig.
55), though whether the influence went from the mainland to Cyprus or in
the reverse direction we cannot tell. There are two further links with Cyprus in the discovery at Tarsus of some fragments and a whole pot of
Erimi style (Schaeffer, 1936, pp. 20 ff., Pl. V; 1948, p. 577, No. 237, Fig.
313) and a curious black and red streak-polished ware, which, as far as
we know, has been found only at Tarsus in Cilicia, and there only in small
quantity, and in Cyprus (pottery from Kyra Alonia; information kindly supplied by the excavator, Dr. Porphyrios Dikaios), where Dr. Dikaios has
called it "combed ware."

A stronger link with Anatolia exists in the plain red-burnished wares,
especially in a small jar with four vertically pierced tubular lugs, of which
Tarsus produced only a fragmentary example but which is undoubtedly the
same as shape C31 of Troy I (Blegen, Caskey, Rawson, and Sperling, 1950,
Fig. 131b) and Thermi I and later (Lamb, 1936, Fig. 26, class A, pyxis
form 1). In the group of plain light clay red-slipped wares there is also a
cup shape with a characteristic drooping handle paralleled in a single example at Polatli (Lloyd and Gökçe, 1951, p. 41, Fig. 9., group 10, 7) in central Anatolia, where it belongs, however, to a cooking pot, and again at
Amuq H in Syria.

Finally, corrugated light clay ware, sometimes of a greenish color
and chiefly of goblet shape (Fig. 1, b), forms a further link with Amuq H-I.

---

eastern and Central Europe" to draw attention to a possible Danubian
parallel (see Ehrich, p. 117, below).

The best specimens are probably imported Syrian ware (Braidwood, 1940, p. 216, Fig. 20, 5). A single example of spiral-burnished ware seems again an importation of such jars as were found in Tomb 4 at Qatna (Du Mesnil du Buisson, 1935, pp. 148 f., Pl. XLIII, 208).

For positive, not relative, dating there is an important link with Egypt in pitchers of light clay reserved-slip ware of Cilician type found in a tomb in the Giza Necropolis and dated 2640 B.C. (Reisner, 1942, p. 411, Fig. 234c), according to the chronology given in the handbook of the Boston Museum of Fine Arts, Ancient Egypt (3d ed.; 1952). This is undoubtedly an export from Cilicia. There is a further connection between Egypt and Cilicia in a button seal (Fig. 1, c) of stone covered with light-blue glaze, with handle in animal form (Brunton, 1927, Pl. XXXIII, 114; Metropolitan Museum No. .04.2.174, unpublished). The pattern, consisting of lizard, bull, and prostrate man, is characteristic in its syntax of a group of Egyptian seals which are thought to be of a shape foreign to Egypt and of Asiatic origin. As a group, they come from the later years of the Old Kingdom and the First Intermediate Level (Frankfort, 1926, pp. 88 ff.). The seal belongs to the end of Early Bronze II or the beginnings of Early Bronze III (see Kantor, p. 10, above).

The resemblances between some of the Early Bronze II pottery of Cilicia and that of eastern Crete, where, too, the same type of button seal has been found (Xanthoudídes, 1924, Pls. XIII-XV; Matz, 1928, Pls. XXII-XXIII) is very strong in such shapes as the steep-walled cup (Fig. 1, d), more characteristic of Early Bronze I (Pendlebury and Money-Coutts, 1935-36, pp. 59 ff., Fig. 14), the droop-handled cup (Fig. 1, e) (ibid., p. 49, Fig. 11, 311), although the shape of the bowl of the Cretan cups is not always the same as that of Cilicia, and, in general, in pitcher shapes (ibid., Pls. 11-12). Here the link is not precisely with Cilicia but with a somewhat more western Anatolian type. The Cilician pitcher with rising spout is characterized by a leaf-shaped mouth tapering toward a slightly beaked and drooping pour channel. The more western type, to which many of the eastern Crete pitchers belong, has a troughlike mouth with a squared end.

Early Bronze III

Early Bronze III brings the sudden and overwhelming influx of Trojan shapes; not only the two-handled cup, including Schliemann's original Depas Amphikypellon (Goldman and Garstang, Pls. XCII, 1, 2; XCIII, 1-4; Blegen, Caskey, Rawson, and Sperling, Fig. 129, Troy shapes A42-46), is found in

great numbers and in at least as great diversity of shapes and fabrics as
at Troy itself, but simpler shapes as well are paralleled, such as the shallow bowls with heavy wheelmarks (Fig. 1, f) (Troy shape A2); one-handled
bowls (Fig. 1, g) (Troy shape A11, 21); lids (Fig. 1, h) (Troy shape D1).
Toward the end of Early Bronze III there are high-necked jars (Fig. 1, i)
(Troy shapes C28, 29, etc.), red-cross bowls (Blegen, Caskey, and Rawson,
Fig. 240, 32.69), gold earrings (Schliemann, 1881, pp. 460 ff., Nos. 691,
695, 699, 754-64; Goldman, 1940, Fig. 14), and slitted bronze blades (Schliemann, 1881, p. 499, No. 901; Goldman, 1940, Fig. 19). The numerous in-
trusive pits which appear at Troy for the first time in Troy IId (Blegen,
Caskey, Rawson, and Sperling, 1950, p. 206) also make a sudden appearance at Tarsus in the beginnings of Early Bronze III. Certain architectural
similarities cannot be developed within the space of this paper. The time
range of these parallels is from Troy IIc or d, through Troy IV and, on the
evidence of the red-cross bowls and a few other vessels, possibly into
the beginnings of Troy V.

Central Anatolia.—There is a small body of material comparable in
shape and fabric to the Copper Age wares of Central Anatolia and especially of Polatli, where, also, the two-handled cup of Trojan type was found
(Lloyd and Gökçe, 1951, p. 42, Fig. 10, 24). Typical shapes are the bowl
or dipper with high-swung handle (Fig. 1, j) (ibid., p. 39, Fig. 8, group 7),
the cup with horned handle (Fig. 1, k) (ibid., p. 40, Fig. 9, group 10, 2),
slipped and burnished bowls with grooved and fluted decoration (ibid., p.
47, Fig. 11, groups 28-29).

An even smaller number of sherds—a mere handful—show closer resemblance to Khirbet Kerak. They have the contrasts of red and black or
buff and black between exterior body and rim, the rim color being identical
with that of the interior. The black fragments, two in number, have a splen-
did jetlike brilliance. One cannot, however, speak of a Khirbet Kerak period. In Cilicia the large, heavy ribbed vessels are not represented at all,
and the conclusions reached by Mrs. Amiran (1952, pp. 89 ff.) seem to me
sound. It is perhaps significant, however, that these sherds should appear
well within the Early Bronze III strata. She considers the Copper Age
wares of Central Anatolia, with their channeled and grooved surfaces, related to, but not identical with, Khirbet Kerak, "at least a second grade relationship between the makers and the Anatolian population." The teapot
shape of Polatli (Lloyd and Gökçe, 1951, p. 33) appears for the first time
in Early Bronze III in a red-slipped and burnished ware. It has its great-

est development in the dark-on-light wares of Middle Bronze and persists into Hittite levels.

Toward the very end of Early Bronze III a new wave of influence starts from Syria; and, as it appears at the moment when there is evidence of destruction, I think it likely that it was brought by invaders, possibly Hurrians, whose historic appearance in Mesopotamia is now held to have started in the second half of the third millennium (Speiser, 1931-32, pp. 13 ff.). They bring the caliciform (Fig. 1, 1) wares of Amuq J and Hama J (Ingholt, 1940, p. 35, Pl. XI, 2). A fragment with typical scrabble pattern found in Middle Bronze context is probably an imported Syrian bit (Ingholt, 1940, p. 35, Pl. XI, 2). There are also typical dark-clay spiral-burnished bottles (Fig 1, m) of Syrian type (Woolley, 1913-14, Pls. XXIII, 12-13) and the comb-incised two-handled jars (Fig. 1, n) known from both Syria and Palestine (Albright, 1930-31, pp. 8 f., Pls. 3, 9-13; 4, 37, 43, 44, 48; 5, 12-14; 7, 11-29). Other of the Early Bronze wares, such as the red-washed bowls, are also related to Palestine, but both Palestine and Cilicia probably received them from Syria. Pottery with stamp-seal impressions also has its Syrian parallels at Hama (Hama J) (Ingholt, 1940, Pls. XIV, XV, 1-2; Goldman, 1940, Fig. 27).

Middle Bronze

The beginnings of Middle Bronze continue in the first meter of deposit a few of the wares and shapes that are characteristic of late Early Bronze III: seal-stamped pottery, bottles, comb-decorated jars, red-cross bowls; but the new types of dark-on-light painted ware of Syrian affiliation make their appearance simultaneously. Light clay wares either painted or plain are the hallmark of Cilician Middle Bronze. A high-pedestaled bowl (Fig. 1, o) found at Tarsus is a unique shape and is best paralleled in Iran (noted by Welker, 1948, p. 209, Pl. V, 29); but, as this shape had already come into existence in Hissar Ia (Herzfeld, 1941, pp. 97 f., Fig. 192; Schmidt, 1937, Pl. III, H5196, H1522) and is still found in a more sophisticated form in Tepe Giyan II (Contenau and Ghirshman, 1935, Pl. 21, tomb 64), it has little value for purposes of chronology. A bronze spearhead with heavy midrib and bent knobbed tang also points toward Iran (Hissar III) (Schmidt, 1937, Pl. L, H3582; Goldman, 1938, Fig. 14), but a closer parallel comes from Syria itself (Schaeffer, 1939-40, Pl. XXIII, 1). Direct influence from Iran seems to me unlikely and almost impossible, should the high dating of Hissar III suggested by McCown be maintained (McCown, 1942, pp. 50 ff.,

62; see Foreword, p. ix, and McCown, p. 61 above).

The most characteristic Syrian parallels are with Ras Shamra Level II, Hama H, Atchana VII and earlier levels, and Mishrifé Qatna, especially in the numerous trefoil-mouthed painted "eye" pitchers (Fig. 1, p) (Schaeffer, 1939-40, p. 283, Fig. 5, L-M; Du Mesnil du Buisson, 1927, pp. 13 ff., Fig. 47, Pls. VIII, XI, 1; Woolley, 1947, Figs. 10, 12, 14) and small bowls (Fig. 1, q) (Schaeffer, 1948, p. 267, refers to similar pottery, not illustrated). In small bowls Cilicia shows perhaps a greater preference for the pedestaled type; on the other hand, the frequent animal motifs found on the painted Syrian ware (Woolley, 1947, Figs. 10, 14) are infrequent in Cilicia. The early wares have neat and simple patterns, including butterfly or hourglass triangles in metope arrangement. Later the decoration tends to become more careless and suggests characteristic Khabur ware (Mallowan, 1937, Pl. 21, 9-10; Speiser, 1935, Pl. LXX, 144). It seems likely that the beginnings of dark-on-light ware in Cilicia postdate its first appearance at Atchana and antedate the version characteristic of the Khabur region. There are a very few, probably imported, fragments of what Braidwood calls smeared wash ware (Amuq J).

Cypriote connections are confined to a few fragments of imported red-on-black and red-on-red Middle Bronze Cypriote ware (Gjerstad, pp. 177 f.).

Late Bronze I

In spite of the fact that the Middle Bronze period ended with considerable destruction, many elements of the culture persisted, although they gradually took on quite a different form. One recognizes at once in the recrudescence of monochrome slipped wares and in new pottery shapes the arrival of new elements from the Hittite region. These correspond in type to the pottery of the Older Hittite Empire. For this reason and also because the time must be about 1600 B.C., when the Late Bronze Age begins elsewhere, it seems best to call this new cultural phase "Late Bronze I." Some scholars (Schaeffer, 1948; Bittel, 1950, p. 25), however, who have dealt with the Bronze Age at Tarsus on the basis of the preliminary reports and "A Conspectus of Early Cilician Pottery," which have appeared in the American Journal of Archeology, have referred to it as the "later phase of Middle Bronze." This, in my opinion, does not do justice to the really novel character of the period and the historic implications of the Hittite contacts so definitely illustrated by the now famous seal of Isputahsuh, the king of Kizzuwatna, which was found in the upper layers of Late Bronze I.

In general, the divisions made by the excavators in the Cilician material are based upon innovations rather than upon the continuation of older types.

Certain shapes of the dark-on-light Middle Bronze wares now disappear, such as the small pedestaled bowl and, with a very few exceptions, the trefoil-mouthed "eye" jug. Large bowls with painted rims persist. There are still a few examples of the Khabur-type jar, and then it, too, is no longer found. The dark-on-light ware gradually evolves into a polychrome style with wavy-line patterns not unlike pottery known best from Palestine (Tufnell, Inge, and Harding, 1940, Pl. XLIX, 261). There are new shapes, judging by the small and rather fragmentary body of material. There is a single example of the "Ajjul" type of vase with bird panel (Heurtley, 1938, Pl. XX). As a result of the direct influences from the Older Hittite Empire, monochrome red polished ware is found in increasing quantity. The shapes include: trefoil-mouthed red-slipped and burnished pitchers with mammiform bosses (Von der Osten, 1937, p. 138, Fig. 182); the large square Hittite "bathtub" (Fig. 1, r) with interior shelf (ibid., p. 190, Fig. 205, d1766); fragments of the urnlike teapots (ibid., p. 138, Fig. 192, d2267) and a great variety of typical Hittite spouts (ibid., Figs. 225 f.); large partially glazed bowls with two or four handles (Fig. 1, s) (Von der Osten, 1937, Figs. 170-71). To this must be added the first appearance of the Hittite type of bulla.

Of first importance among new Syrian types is the black to gray Atchana impressed ware (Fig. 1, t) (Alalakh publication not available to writer). The shapes, however, in so far as preliminary publications of Atchana have shown us the material, are, with the exception of fragments of wide goblet or beaker rims, quite different at Tarsus. The chief shape at Tarsus is the typical Syrian spindle jug. Included among the ornamental elements of impressed rosette, incised star, and so forth, already known from Atchana, is the tree placed between antithetic goats. This motif is very reminiscent of cylinder seals, although it also appears on pottery (Frankfort, 1939, Pls. XXXII C, XLII O; Contenau, 1922, Pl. XXXIV, 240; Tufnell, Inge, and Harding, 1940, Pl. XLVIII, 250). Mr. G. F. Swift kindly informs me by letter that spindle flasks were found in this ware, although without animal motif and without white fill, in the Amuq region explored by Braidwood. It is puzzling that Cilicia should produce on a Syrian shape a Syrian motif not yet found in that region itself. This may well be due to chance. There is no evidence at all at Tarsus for the occurrence of the Tell

Judeideh juglet with pricked design, which has been associated with the
Hyksos.

Late Bronze II

Although there is a slight continuation of partially slipped and burnished ware, the bulk of the Hittite wares of this period are the plain ones
of either a buff or a reddish tinge. The Late Bronze II is definitely divided into two periods. In Period LB IIa, a large temple of Hittite type was
built on the summit of the hill in Section A (Bossert, 1942, p. 92), and in
Section B a large building which must have been either a rather modest
palace for the local Hittite ruler or an administrative building. In connection with the latter were found most of the Hittite bullae giving the names
of a number of princes and the royal seal of Pu-du-hepa (Goldman, 1937,
pp. 280 f., Fig. 40; Goetze, 1937, p. 287; Gelb, 1937, pp. 289 ff.). In the
same connection there was a land deed conforming in language and character to those found at Bogaz Köy (Goetze, 1939, pp. 1 ff.). All this is very
strong evidence for the complete Hittite control of Tarsus and undoubtedly
most of Cilicia. Period A ended in destruction.

Period B, the second period of Late Bronze II, is characterized by
much more modest architecture and by the sudden appearance of granary
style Mycenaean pottery (LM IIIc 1). The catastrophe which ended Phase
A took place sometime in the last quarter of the thirteenth century and is
only another one of the many which overwhelmed the Mediterranean fringe
of the Near East at that time. There is no difference between the Hittite
type of pottery of Late Bronze IIa and that of Late Bronze IIb, so that no
interval when the site was uninhabited, or at least none of any length, can
be postulated. The shapes include typical pitchers (Koşay, 1951, Pl. XLV);
large and small shallow, carelessly made bowls (Von der Osten, 1937, Fig.
167, c. 272, d2678); numberless miniature bowls and jugs (Koşay, 1951,
Pls. XLII, 1, LXII); lentoid jugs, large and small (Bossert, 1942, p. 148,
No. 633); and large jugs with pointed base (Koşay, 1951, Pl. L, 1-2).

Imports from or parallels with Syria include the lentoid jug with at-
tached pot-stand (Bossert, 1951, pp. 222, 752) and certain forms of amphorae (ibid., pp. 223, 759).

In Late Bronze IIa there is a very small importation of white-slip
Cypriote II ware, such as was found in quantities in Syria, and a single
example of a Cypriote monochrome ware bowl. The Mycenaean pottery
of Late Bronze IIb includes a considerable number of imported vessels as

well as those made locally, and the importations show a direct connection with the Greek mainland (Broneer, 1933 and 1939, passim; Wace, 1921-23, passim).

Toward the end of Late Bronze IIb a ware with red painted designs on a reddish-buff clay makes its first appearance. This type of ware has a wide distribution and is found with slight variations in Syria, Palestine, and Cyprus. In ornament it shows many Mycenaean survivals, although there are new and un-Mycenaean shapes. This pottery, however, is really part of the Iron Age and will not be discussed here.

Table 1
The Relative Chronology of Southeastern Anatolia
(This table emphasizes only the major correlations of Cilicia)

	Anatolia							Greece		
Cilicia	Kültepe	Polatli	Alishar	Bogazköy	Alaca	Kusura	Troy	Mainland Greece	Crete	Cyprus
Neolithic										
Early and Transitional Chalcolithic										
Middle Chalcolithic										
Late Chalcolithic										
Early Bronze I							Id and later (scored ware)	Leaf-impressed pithos base		
Early Bronze II							I (pyxis shape)		East Crete	Erimi; Early Bronze; general resemblance of incised patterns; Kyra Alonia
Early Bronze III		Phases I and II					Possible range IIc-early V			
Middle Bronze	IV (imported Syro-Cilician ware)									Red on black and red on red Middle Cypriote ware imported into Cilicia
Late Bronze I	I	Phase IV	Hittite phase	IV later phase	II	C				
Late Bronze IIa			Hittite phase	III	II					Late Cypriote II
Late Bronze IIb								Mycenaean granary style		

Table 1 (continued)

Amuq	Ras Shamra	Mishrifé Qatna	Atchana	Qalat-er-Rus	Hama	Jericho	Beit Mersim	Lachish	Hassuna	Tepe Gawra	Egypt	Europe
A-B	V				M	X-XVII						
D-E	IV-III									XIX-XII		
D-E	III				L?					XIA-IX		
F	III			19-17	K?					XIA-IX		
G; a few general resemblances; little specific				13								
H-I		Tomb 4									Imported Egyptian seal at Tarsus; Old Kingdom, transitional period; imported Cilician pottery in Egyptian tomb ca. 2640 B.C.	Danubian Bandkeramik? (see Ehrich)
J	--------II-1				J	H						
L	II	"Eye pitcher," etc.	VII and earlier levels		H							
	Ugarit Recent 1		V VI					Fosse Temple				
	Ugarit Recent 2, 3											

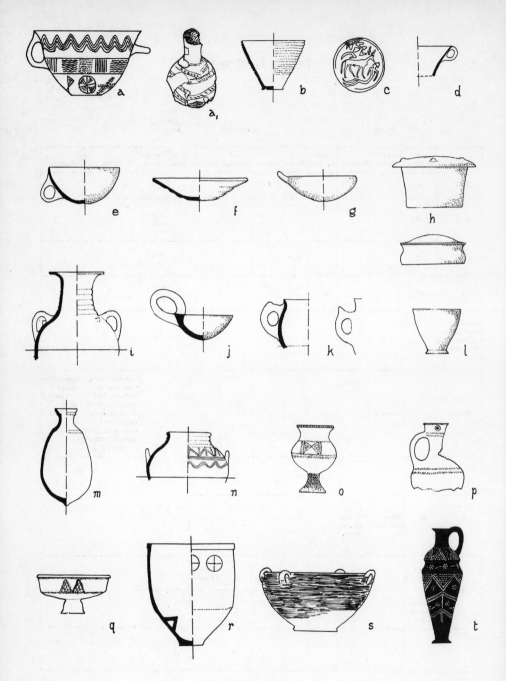

Figure 1

References

Albright, W. F. "The Excavation of Tell Beit Mirsim in Palestine: The Pottery of the First Three Campaigns," Annual of the American Schools of Oriental Research, XII (1930-31), 1 ff.

Amiran, R. B. K. "Connections between Anatolia and Palestine in the Early Bronze Age," Israel Exploration Journal, II (1952), 89 ff.

Bittel, K. "Zur Chronologie der anatolischen Frühkulturen," Reinecke Festschrift, ed. G. Behrens and J. Werner. Mainz: E. Schneider, 1950.

Blegen, C. W.; Caskey, J. L.; Rawson, M.; and Sperling, J. Troy: General Introduction, the First and Second Settlements. Princeton, N. J.: Princeton University Press, 1950.

Blegen, C. W.; Caskey, J. L.; and Rawson, M. Troy: The Third, Fourth, and Fifth Settlements. Princeton, N. J.: Princeton University Press, 1951.

Bossert, H. Th. Altanatolien. Berlin: Ernst Wasmuth, 1942.

_____. Altsyrien. Tübingen: Verlag Ernst Wasmuth, 1951.

Braidwood, R. J. "Report on Two Sondages on the Coast of Syria, South of Tartous," Syria, XXI (1940), 183 ff.

Broneer, O. "Excavations on the North Slope of the Acropolis," Hesperia, II (1933), 329 ff.

_____. "A Mycenaean Fountain on the Athenian Acropolis," ibid., VIII (1939), 317 ff.

Brunton, G. Qau and Badari, I. London: British School of Archaeology in Egypt and Egyptian Research Account, 1927.

Contenau, G. La Glyptique syro-hittite. Paris: Paul Geuthner, 1922.

Contenau, G., and Ghirshman, R. Fouilles de Tépé Giyan près de Néhavend, 1931 et 1932. Paris: Libraire orientaliste Paul Geuthner, 1935.

Du Mesnil du Buisson. "Les Ruines d'el Mishrifé," Syria, VIII (1927), 13 ff.

_____. Le Site archéologique de Mishrifé-Qatna. Paris: Libraire Orientaliste Paul Geuthner, 1935.

Ehrich, A. M. H. Early Pottery of the Jebeleh Region. ("Memoirs of the American Philosophical Society," Vol. XIII.) Philadelphia, 1939.

Frankfort, H. "Egypt and Syria in the First Intermediate Period," Journal of Egyptian Archaeology, XII (1926), 80 ff.

_____. Cylinder Seals. London: Macmillan & Co., Ltd., 1939.

Garstang, J. "Explorations in Cilicia," Liverpool Annals of Archaeology and Anthropology, XXIV (1937), 52 ff.

_____. "Explorations in Cilicia," ibid., XXV (1938), 71 ff.

_____. "Explorations in Cilicia," ibid., XXVI (1938), 38 ff., 89 ff.

_____. Prehistoric Mersin. Oxford: Oxford University Press, 1953.

Garstang, J.; Phythian-Adams, W. J.; Seton-Williams, V. "Third Report on the Excavations at Sakje-Geuzi, 1908-1911," Liverpool Annals of Archaeology and Anthropology, XXIV (1937), 119 ff.

Gelb, I. J. "Queen Pudu-Ḫepa," American Journal of Archaeology, XLI (1937), 289-91.

Gjerstad, E. Studies on Prehistoric Cyprus. Uppsala, 1926.

Goetze, A. "Remarks on the Epigraphic Material Found at Tarsus in 1936," American Journal of Archaeology, XLI (1937), 287-88.

_____. "Cuneiform Inscriptions from Tarsus," Journal of the American Oriental Society, LIX (1939), 1-16.

Goldman, H. "Preliminary Expedition to Cilicia, 1934, and Excavations at Gözlu Kule, Tarsus, 1935," American Journal of Archaeology, XXXIX (1935), 526 ff.

_____. "Excavations at Gözlu Kule, Tarsus, 1936," ibid., XLI (1937), 262 ff.

_____. "Excavations at Gözlu Kule, Tarsus, 1937," ibid., XLII (1938), 30 ff.

_____. "Excavations at Gözlu Kule, Tarsus, 1938," ibid., XLIV (1940), 60 ff.

Goldman, H., and Garstang, J. "A Conspectus of Early Cilician Pottery," American Journal of Archaeology, LI (1947), 370 ff.

Herzfeld, E. E. Iran in the Ancient East. London: Oxford University Press, 1941.

Heurtley, W. A. "A Palestinian Vase-Painter of the Sixteenth Century B.C.," Quarterly of the Department of Antiquities in Palestine, VIII (1938), 21 ff.

Ingholt, H. Rapport préliminaire sur sept campagnes de fouilles à Hama en Syrie. Copenhagen: Ejnar Muksgaard, 1940.

Kenyon, K. M. "Excavations at Jericho, 1952," Palestine Exploration Quarterly (1952), pp. 62 ff.

Koşay, H. Z. Les Fouilles d'Alaça Hoyuk, 1937-39. ("Publications de la Société d'Histoire Turque.") Ankara, 1951.

Lamb, W. Excavations at Thermi in Lesbos. Cambridge: At the University Press, 1936.

Lloyd, S., and Gökçe, N. "Excavations at Polatli," Anatolian Studies, I (1951), 21 ff.

Luschan, F. von. Die Kleinfunde von Sendschirli. ("Mitteilungen aus den orientalischen Sammlungen," Vol. XV.) Berlin, 1943.

McCown, D. E. The Comparative Stratigraphy of Iran. ("Oriental Institute of the University of Chicago Studies in Oriental Civilization," Vol. XXIII.) Chicago: University of Chicago Press, 1942.

Mallowan, E. L. "The Excavations at Tall Chagar Bazar and an Archaeological Survey of the Habur Region. Second Campaign, 1936," Iraq, IV (1937), 91 ff.

Matz, F. Die frühkretischen Siegel. Berlin and Leipzig: Walter de Gruyter & Co., 1928.

Ormerod, H. A. "Prehistoric Remains in Southwestern Asia Minor," Annual of the British School at Athens, XVI (1909-10), 76 ff.; XVIII (1911-12), 80 ff.; XIX (1912-13), 48 ff.

Osten, H. H. von der. The Alishar Hüyük Seasons of 1930-32, Part II. Chicago: University of Chicago Press, 1937.

Pendlebury, H. W. and J. D. S., and Money-Coutts, M. B. "Excavations in the Plain of Lasithi. I. The Cave of Trapeza," Annual of the British School at Athens, XXXVI (1935-36), 5-131.

Perkins, A. The Comparative Archaeology of Early Mesopotamia. Chicago: University of Chicago Press, 1949.

Pumpelly, R. Explorations in Turkestan: Prehistoric Civilizations of Anau. Washington, D.C.: Carnegie Institution of Washington, 1908.

Reisner, G. A. A History of the Giza Necropolis. Cambridge: Harvard University Press, 1942.

Schaeffer, C. F. A. Missions en Chypre 1932-35. Paris: Libraire orientaliste Paul Geuthner, 1936.

_____. "X^e et XIe campagnes de fouilles à Ras Shamra-Ugarit," Syria, XX (1939-40), 36 ff.

_____. Stratigraphie comparée et chronologie de l'Asie occidentale, IIIe et IIe millénaires. London: Oxford University Press, 1948.

Schliemann, H. Ilios: The City and Country of the Trojans. New York: Harper & Bros., 1881.

Schmidt, E. F. Excavations at Tépé Hissar, Damghan. Philadelphia: University of Pennsylvania Press, 1937.

Speiser, E. A. "Ethnic Movements in the Near East in the Second Millennium B.C.," Annual of the American Schools of Oriental Research, XIII (1931-32), 13 ff.

_____. Excavations at Tepe Gawra, Vol. I. Philadelphia: University of Pennsylvania Press, 1935.

Tufnell, O.; Inge, C. H.; and Harding, L. Lachish, Vol. II: The Fosse Temple. London: Oxford University Press, 1940.

Wace, A. J. B. "Excavations at Mycenae," Annual of the British School at Athens, Vol. XXV (1921-23).

Welker, M. "The Painted Pottery of the Near East in the Second Millennium B.C. and Its Chronological Background," Transactions of the American Philosophical Society, XXXVIII (1948), 185 ff.

Woolley, C. L. "Hittite Burial Customs," Liverpool Annals of Archaeology and Anthropology, VI (1913-14), 87 ff.

Woolley, L. "The Tomb of Yarim-Lin," Illustrated London News, October 25, 1947, pp. 470 ff.

Xanthoudídes, X. The Vaulted Tombs of the Mesará. Translated by J. P. Droop. London: University of Liverpool Press, 1924.

The Relative Chronology of the Aegean in the
Neolithic Period and the Early Bronze Age

Saul S. Weinberg
University of Missouri

The reliability of the chronology of any prehistoric culture and of the
relative chronology of successive cultures varies in direct proportion to
the area excavated in the stratified sites and to the nature of the strata
themselves; it is likely to vary in inverse proportion to the age of those
excavations, though modern excavators do not always improve on the methods of those of one and two generations ago. It is therefore necessary to
preface the following scheme of Aegean chronology with a brief statement
on the age and nature of the excavations from which were derived the materials on which it is based. Starting in the north, the prehistory of Macedonia is known chiefly from a series of pit diggings in mounds, made largely by the British in the 1920's, with a more sizable area opened at Servia
(Heurtley, 1939, pp. 43-56). In the same decade a considerable area of
the Neolithic site at Olynthus was laid bare (Mylonas, 1929), and both this
and the British excavations were published fully. Preliminary notices of
the trial excavations at Akropotamos and Polystylo in eastern Macedonia
in 1938 offer promising new material (Mylonas, 1941). Of various other
Greek excavations there are no adequate reports. So we have but a scrap-
py picture of Macedonian prehistory, based mainly on a pottery sequence
obtained in pits and with no idea of the culture as a whole. Yet the region
promises excellent material in innumerable high mounds, which the pits
show to offer good stratigraphy and deep layers; but they await excavation
on a large scale.

For Thessaly there is reliable information from well-stratified and
well-published sites excavated in fairly large areas in the first decade of
this century (Tsountas, 1908; Wace and Thompson, 1912); there was almost no excavation from 1912 to 1952, but work is beginning again. Consequently, we have a good picture that is forty years old, but no up-to-
date knowledge of stratigraphy. Again, there are plentiful opportunities
for excavation on a scale sufficient to check and rectify our ideas of Thessalian prehistory, and it is hoped that the new excavations will be suffi-

ciently comprehensive to provide this check.

We have no reliable information on the stratigraphy of the Neolithic period in central Greece, though there is much material from fine mounds tested in the first decade of this century and the possibilities for further work are excellent. The report on the Halae Neolithic pottery might improve the situation. For the Bronze Age we are somewhat better off, thanks to the fine excavation and publication of Eutresis in Boeotia (Goldman, 1931), the stratification of which forms the basis for sorting out the Early Helladic material known from other sites in the region. Kirrha in Phocis yielded stratified Early Helladic remains and perhaps even Neolithic, but they are not yet published. Attica, too, provides little or no stratified Neolithic and but one stratified Early Helladic site, Haghios Kosmas (Mylonas, 1934), published only preliminarily. The wells in the Athenian Agora contained good closed groups of both periods, which will be useful when the stratigraphy is clear. Very recent excavations by Theochares at several places in Attica are helping to clarify the picture somewhat, but these are still on a very small scale and not yet in deep ac-cumulations with good stratigraphy.

In the Peloponnesus the excavator of prehistoric remains is often con-fronted with a peculiar situation which has not been appreciated generally. Rocky outcrops were chosen more often than low knolls for Neolithic sites, with the result that there are few mounds, and these are very low. The strata on most sites tend to be much more shallow than those of settle-ments to the north, especially in the Neolithic levels. But if the lines of division are not always sharp and clear, the general succession is une-quivocal, and the scheme of relative chronology much better established than in central Greece, though not so clear as in Thessaly. Corinthia and the Argolid are best known, while single published sites represent Arcadia (Holmberg, 1944) and Messenia (Valmin, 1938) in both the Neolithic and Early Helladic periods. The third phase of the latter period is very well known from well-stratified sites in the Argolid and Corinthia, but Early Helladic I and II are still known largely from pits. The new excavations at Lerna promise to alleviate this situation. For both periods there is much unpublished material, the knowledge of which would help greatly with interrelations and chronology.

In no section of the Aegean is there such poverty of reliable informa-tion amid such plenty of material as in the Cyclades. Whether or not there was a Neolithic occupation is not known, but the Early Bronze Age material is copious. Unfortunately, it is largely from tombs, Phylakopi on Melos being the only settlement excavated on any scale (Phylakopi, 1904). The excavations are largely fifty years old or more, and it is only quite recently that renewed work in the Cyclades is producing fresh material. There is, however, every indication that these islands early occupied a focal position on the trade and migration routes, and excavation of stratified sites is urgently needed. There has recently been more work on the islands along the Asia Minor coast, on Chios, Lesbos, Lemnos, and Samos, with Neolithic material coming from the first and last, but not stratified, and Early Bronze material from all of them. Only Thermi on Lesbos is fully published (Lamb, 1936); but the Heraion site on Samos promises good stratigraphy, as does Poliochni on Lemnos. There is still much to be done, and we know relatively little.

Despite the deep stratigraphy on the Knossos mound, we know little of the Cretan Neolithic because so little has been published. However, a new study of the material in the stratigraphic museum on the site is forthcoming and promises valuable information; excavation on a larger scale is very necessary. Meanwhile, deep Neolithic layers have appeared within the last two years at Phaistos (Levi, 1952), and much material was found in the Lasithi (Pendlebury, 1935-36) just before the last war, but this was very late, even sub-Neolithic. Recent excavations in western Crete help fill out the picture, but still the only stratified site covering the entire Neolithic development is Knossos (Evans, 1921-35, I, 32-55; II, 1-21), which must remain the framework for Cretan Neolithic. The Early Minoan period is much better known; yet there is a lack of good stratigraphy on any one site covering the whole phase, and its first subperiod is especially vague. There is thus still the possibility of much disagreement on questions of relative chronology in Crete, which only selective excavation will eliminate.

It is clear, then, that prehistoric excavation and research, especially for the earlier phases being considered here, has lagged far behind almost every other branch of Greek archeology; that for almost every region of the Aegean our knowledge is based on excavations either too old or too limited; that a large percentage of the material we have is not from stratified sites; or that the stratigraphy, when present, has not been observed, largely because the excavations are so old. How, then, you might ask, is it possible to build a scheme of relative chronology with any confidence in its reliability? The answer lies in the minority of well-stratified, well-excavated sites, which for most regions offer the basis for a chronological scheme, even if there be but one good site; all the rest of the material must be built around that framework. True, this does not instil perfect confidence; but the actual state of Greek prehistory has been outlined here to emphasize the tentative nature of our scheme, to point out its strength and weaknesses, and especially to highlight the necessity for new and large-scale excavations on well-stratified sites in every region of the Aegean. Truly, Aegean prehistory is in its infancy as a science.

Nevertheless, there are certain well-established facts which you can accept with confidence and which form a firm, if meager, basis for a relative chronology of the Neolithic period and the Early Bronze Age (Weinberg, 1947). The much less problematical Middle and Late Bronze Ages are left aside here, for their chronologies are largely clear cut, well established, and well known. There is, too, a rather sharp break between Early and Middle Bronze in most parts of the Aegean, which makes a convenient terminus for us here, for the development which begins after this break runs uninterruptedly to the end of prehistoric times. Fortunately, also, one of the best comparative links we have between the Aegean and the Near East comes immediately before this break and so allows us to establish its position in the relative scheme of both regions with little doubt. I refer to the "red-cross bowls," which usually have a red band about the inside of the lip and a cross in the same red paint or glaze on the interior of the bowl (Fig. 1, 1). At several sites in the Peloponnesus and central Greece these bowls occur in fairly large numbers in the Early Helladic III levels and as part of the latest development of that phase (Blegen, 1921, p. 6, Fig. 53; 1928, p. 83, Fig. 69; Kunze, 1934, p. 65; Lemerle, 1937, p. 460, Fig. 23; Valmin, 1938, p. 277, Pl. XVII, 62), just before the destruction which generally marks the break between Early and Middle Helladic. On the other side of the Aegean, the occurrence of identical bowls is limited at Troy to the end of Settlement IV and through V (Blegen, Caskey, and Rawson, 1951, pp. 138, 236, 250-51, Figs. 240, 246). The trail runs through Anatolia, where the bowls occur at Kusura in the transition from Phase B to Phase C (Lamb, 1938, p. 245, Fig. 14, 13). At Polatli, in central Anatolia, they come from Levels 11-15 (Lloyd and Gökçe, 1951, p. 46, Fig. 5, type No. 26), clearly equated by many features with Troy IV and V. At the eastern end of the line, the bowls are found at Tarsus at the end of the Early Bronze III level (Goldman, 1940, p. 65; Goldman and Garstang, 1947, p. 384, Pl. XCIII, 10; see also Goldman, p. 74, above), a position identical with that in Greece. The single example, not several, from a Late Hittite level at Mersin (Garstang, 1939-40, p. 132) would seem to be out of context. There can be little doubt of the contemporaneity of the end of the Early Bronze Age along this whole northern border of the eastern Mediterranean. There is a unique link which connects the Greek mainland in the Early Helladic III period directly with Egypt of the Eleventh Dynasty; that is the seal impression on a jar from Asine (Fig. 1, 2) (Frödin and Persson, 1938, p. 217, No. 15, Fig. 160, 1-2), of a type which in Egypt does not outlast Dynasty XI (Matz, 1940, p. 152).

For Crete, it is clear that the Middle Minoan phase began during Dynasty XI (Pendlebury, 1939, p. 122), while the Early Minoan III seals, it is generally agreed, cover the range from the end of Dynasty VI into Dynasty XI (Matz, 1950, p. 182; see Kantor, p. 10 above). It is possible that some of the Cretan seals related to Egyptian types occur at the end of Early Minoan II (Schachermeyr, 1949-50, p. 25, n. 26), not earlier, which would mean that this period must end within the range of Dynasty VI, which is obvious from other links as well, but not that Early Minoan II must begin within the period of Dynasty VI, as Matz has recently reasoned (Matz, 1950, p. 184). The Early Minoan II stone bowls, of Mochlos especially (Seager, 1912), support an equation of this phase with Dynasties IV-VI (Schachermeyr, 1949-50, p. 25). We have thus equated both Early Helladic III and Early Minoan III with Dynasty XI in Egypt. There has been some dispute, however, as to the relative dates of the end of each of these Aegean phases. Miss Goldman argued over twenty years ago for a close synchronism (Goldman, 1931, p. 233), and nothing discovered since has altered the validity of her reasoning. Since, in the present state of our knowledge, it would be futile to attempt to argue about half-centuries, we can but consider the end of Early Minoan and Early Helladic as roughly contemporary, certainly less than a century apart. There is meager evidence to show, as is logical, that the Early Cycladic phase ended at about the same time. The end of the Early Bronze Age in the Aegean world would thus have occurred by, or only slightly later than, the end of Dynasty XI. The end of Troy V cannot be long, if at all, after; and to about the same date must belong the end of the Early Bronze at Tarsus. The upper terminus of our Aegean scheme is thus well established; future discoveries may result in refinements.

A basic equation for the chronology of the Early Bronze Age in the Aegean is that established by the recent excavators at Troy, where it was shown that Early Helladic pottery occurred from Middle Troy I into Troy V and that some of the imported ware in Middle Troy I "clearly represents the glaze technique usually assigned to the middle phases of the Early Helladic period" (Blegen, Caskey, Rawson, and Sperling, 1950, p. 54). Blegen is here speaking of the Helladic scheme as he and Wace established it on the basis of Peloponnesian stratigraphy, where Early Helladic II begins with the appearance of Urfirnis, or glazed, ware (Wace and Blegen, 1918); at Eutresis, Miss Goldman chose to place the first Urfirnis ware within the Early Helladic I period (Goldman, 1931, pp. 83, 93). At any rate, Early Helladic II must have been established by Middle Troy I, and Early Helladic I lies earlier; Early Helladic II and III cover the span from Middle Troy I to the end of Troy V, or to very near its end, as the red-cross bowls show.

The abundance of so-called "Trojan" pottery types at Polatli (Lloyd and Gökçe, 1951) and at Tarsus has recently made possible a closer integration of Troy I-V with Anatolia and the Near East. The Early Helladic synchronisms will then follow along in their proper sequence. There is, however, one clear link which can be mentioned here, and that is the similarity between the jewelry and vessels of the "treasures" at Troy (Schliemann, 1881, pp. 453-514) and those of the Royal Tombs at Ur (Woolley, 1934) (see Foreword, pp. viii-ix, above). Thanks to the American excavations at Troy, it is now established that it was almost certainly in IIg that the great "treasures" of gold objects were found, to paraphrase Blegen (Blegen, Caskey, Rawson, and Sperling, 1950, p. 207). This implies also a more general identity of Schliemann's "Burnt City," which he first called Troy III, with level IIg; and, since the remains of this level were most abundant, this is an important synchronization. In many features the jewelry and the gold vessels closely resemble those from the Ur tombs, as Dr. Ann Perkins long ago pointed out to me. Still more recently a quadruple spiral silver bead from Brak (Fig. 1, 3) identical with those from Troy IIg (Fig. 1, 4) (Schliemann, 1881, p. 489, 490), was found in a context which dates it "not much before the reign of Naram Sin, or much after the reign of Gimil Sin," to quote Mallowan (1947, pp. 74, 171-76); other such beads come from the Royal Graves of the Copper Age at Alaca Höyük (Fig. 1, 5) (Koşay, 1944, p. 146, Pl. CIX; 1951, Pl. CCVI). The double spiral pins so typical of Troy IIg (Fig. 1, 6) (Schliemann, 1881, p. 489) and found there in the new excavations as well (Blegen, Caskey, Rawson, and Sperling, 1950, p. 367, Pl. 356) also have a parallel at Alaca (Koşay, 1951,

Pls. CXII, 1; CLXXXVII) and are characteristic of Hissar IIb (Fig. 1, 7), continuing into IIIa (Schmidt, 1937, Pls. XXIX, LIV); the Ur tombs offer a double spiral pendant (Woolley, 1934, Pl. 134). Early Helladic and Early Cycladic examples of the pins cannot be placed accurately within the period. The Alaca graves just mentioned must also be brought into this same orbit, for their gold vessels especially, as well as their jewelry, are like those of Troy IIg and Ur. I think, too, that the jewelry of the Early Minoan II tombs at Mochlos is of similar inspiration (Seager, 1912). The whole complex would seem to belong before the end of the Early Dynastic III period in Mesopotamia, certainly before the reign of Naram Sin. There is a sufficient number of parallelisms in pottery shapes and glaze to equate Early Helladic II roughly with Early Minoan II; the beginning of the former has already been shown to fall in the time of Middle Troy I. The immediately preceding phases must then be parallel in part, though they are not necessarily coexistent throughout and there is little to indicate which, if any, lasted longer and began earlier.

The picture with respect to the Early Minoan I phase is complicated by the fact that it apparently came late to Knossos and central Crete, finally displacing a strong sub-Neolithic manifestation; but how much earlier the Bronze Age began in eastern and southern Crete it is difficult to say, owing to the meagerness of excavation in strata of the period. Graves are abundant, but they do not help much when the stratigraphy is in doubt. The sub-Neolithic, strongest in central Crete, has close affinities with what is considered the earliest Cycladic culture; of this we will have more to say later. It has some elements, like pattern-burnishing (Evans, 1921-35, I, 58, Fig. 19), which appear to be Anatolian and can be traced back through Samos (Heidenreich, 1935-36, pp. 128-30, Pls. 41-43, 57, 61-62) and across Anatolia to the Amuq and Sakce Gözü (Taylor, Seton-Williams, Waechter, 1950, pp. 84-85) and which have their counterparts in Neolithic Greece as well. Much has been said of the fragments of stone vessels of Egyptian type found in the uppermost Neolithic level at Knossos (Evans, 1921-35, II, 15-16), and certainly their reliability has been overemphasized and their importance interpreted subjectively (Hutchinson, 1948, p. 62; Matz, 1950, p. 185). A date in Dynasty II or III seems most reasonable, which means that the Early Minoan I manifestation at Knossos, which lies at the end of the Early Minoan I series in general, is concurrent with Dynasty III; we have already equated Early Minoan II with Dynasty IV-VI. However, this does not define the time range of the much stronger and earlier manifestation of Early Minoan I of eastern and southern Crete, which began with the sudden appearance of dark-on-light glaze-painted pottery with globular beaked jug and biconical suspension jug shapes. The beaked jug is characteristically Anatolian, being typical of the Copper Age and occurring from the beginning in Troy I (Blegen, Caskey, Rawson, and Sperling, 1950, pp. 66-67, Fig. 223a), and in the earliest "Anatolian" phase at Tarsus (Goldman and Garstang, 1947, p. 383), but the dark-on-light painted decoration appears late in Anatolia, except in Chalcolithic Mersin in the Halafian orbit. However, one of the Early Minoan I designs is found in white-on-black ware from earliest Kusura (Lamb, 1936a, p. 14, Fig. 6, 13), which is termed "Chalcolithic." So, too, the plug handles of these jugs are Anatolian and occur at least as early as the first phase of Troy I (Blegen, Caskey, Rawson, and Sperling, 1950, p. 65); the same feature occurs in the Amuq phase B, along with the earliest painted pottery there and with pattern-burnished ware. It is probably to this Syro-Anatolian area that one must look for the origins of both the Early Minoan I culture and the partly contemporary sub-Neolithic of Crete; but there are no correlations sufficiently close to give a satisfactory relative date for the movement which brought the Bronze Age to Crete; much more material is needed on the Cretan side and much better stratification. If our correlation for the later part of this phase is correct, its beginning should fall roughly during Dynasties I-II in Egypt, probably not earlier.

On the mainland side, Early Helladic I is no better defined, but the pre-Urfirnis phase must be contemporary with Middle and Early Troy I, though it need not go back as far as the beginning of Troy I. A single striking parallel is offered by a bowl from the lowest meter of deposit at Eutresis (Fig. 1, 10), in which Early Helladic I begins, which has vertical loop handles rising above the lip and is decorated with red glazed bands about the lip and running from lip to base (Goldman, 1931, p. 80, Pl. II). Shape and decorative system occur in the Copper Age chalices at Alishar (Schmidt, 1932, p. 41, Pls. I and VII; Von der Osten, 1937, Pl. VIII), which develop from a concave (Fig. 1, 11) to a convex form (Fig. 1, 12) and would seem to be a development of the bowl shape from Eutresis; the latter is not unlikely an import from central Anatolia, for it is unique and without issue in Greece. Persson compares the earliest Early Helladic vases from Asine (Frödin and Persson, 1938, p. 432) with Alishar and earliest Troy, and it would seem certain that the Greek Bronze Age derives from central and western Anatolia during the Chalcolithic or earliest Copper Age.

Despite the unreliable nature of the information available from the Cyclades, there is every likelihood that the Bronze Age began there even earlier than on the mainland, and perhaps in Crete as well. The mass of material, mostly from graves, has been divided into two groups, the older "Pelos" group, including pottery decorated with rectilinear incised ornament, and the later "Syros" group, with its spiraliform incised decoration and painted pottery (Childe, 1947, pp. 51-35; Frankfort, 1927, pp. 104-9). Yet the Cycladic type of pottery with spiraliform ornament has been found at several Peloponnesian sites (Blegen, 1921, p. 5, Fig. 3: 1928, pp. 76, 212, Pl. IV) and at Eutresis (Goldman, 1931, pp. 80-82, Fig. 97, Pl. III) along with the first Early Helladic pottery, indicating either the source or, more likely, the route of the migration. What is obvious, then, is that this later Cycladic group is clearly as old as the beginnings of the Early Helladic on the mainland, and most likely somewhat older, for the pottery found with the first Early Helladic is well-developed Cycladic pottery of the "Syros" type. The bronze bird-pins of this same group (Fig. 1, 8) (Tsountas, 1899, Pl. 10, 13) are just like those found in Thermi I (Fig. 1, 9) (Lamb, 1936, Pl. XXV), equal to the beginning of Troy I. Therefore, the "Pelos" graves must fall earlier than Troy I and Early Helladic I, and it is not at all strange that a cylinder seal said to be an imitation of a Syrian type of Jemdet Nasr seal should be found in a grave of this group on Amorgos (Frankfort, 1939, pp. 232, 301), for every indication is that the phase is predynastic in date. I have elsewhere shown that there is a group of Cycladic marble seated figurines, of full steatopygous form (Fig. 1, 14), which is the same as figurines of the Middle Neolithic period in both Crete (Fig. 1, 13) and mainland Greece (Weinberg, 1951); they are the immediate ancestors of the more stylized figurines of the "Pelos" graves, some of which still have considerable corporeality, and their antecedents must be sought in the Neolithic and Chalcolithic of Anatolia and the Near East.

Having alluded up to now to the Halafian and pre-Halafian parallels to Greek prehistoric material—and for the steatopygous women there is an excellent one from the Amuq that is called Neolithic (Fig. 1, 16) (Woolley, 1939)—I would make so bold as to suggest here an equation which has been in my mind since 1940 but which seemed impossible until the recent very considerable lowering of Near Eastern dates. I refer to the many Ghassulian features which appear in the earliest Cycladic culture, in the sub-Neolithic and earliest Minoan of Crete, and in the lowest Early Helladic levels, in the mixed Neolithic deposit on Samos. Most striking are the so-called Ghassulian "bird-vases" (Fig. 1, 18) (Mallon, Koeppel, and Neuville, 1934, pp. 107-8, Fig. 57, Pl. 50) of very unusual form which occurs also in the Early Minoan I deposit at Haghios Nikolaos on Crete (Fig. 1, 17) (Evans, 1921-35, I, 60, Fig. 24) as well as in a tomb of the Pyrgos group just excavated near Knossos. This single feature has recently been noticed by Jirku, too (Jirku, 1948). The high-pedestaled feet of the chalices of Samos and the Cretan sub-Neolithic are at Ghassul, too (Mallon, Koeppel, and Neuville, 1934, pp. 105-7, Fig. 56, Pls. 49-50); some bases with holes in them are like earliest Troy I. The propensity to suspension forms and double vertical pierced lugs is common to all these places. Small clay ladles or spoons are characteristic of Early Minoan I at Mochlos (Seager, 1912, Fig. 48, 29-30, 41-42) and occur at Ghassul (Mallon, Koeppel, and Neuville, 1934, p. 104, Fig. 55, Pl. 44). Mat impressions on the bottoms of jars, which would seem to be a very general trait, have, on the contrary, a limited span, occurring in number at Ghassul (Mallon, Koeppel, and Neuville, 1934, pp. 91-92, Pl. 39; Koeppel, 1940, pp. 66-67, Pls. 83-84), in Jericho VIII (Crowfoot, 1938), Megiddo XX (Loud, 1948, Pl. 2, 16-17), all in the late Halaf and Ubaid horizon. They do not occur at Troy; but at near-by Besika Tepe (Lamb, 1932, p. 128) they are associated with pattern-burnishing, both of which are pre-Troy I. The same association occurs on Samos (Heidenreich, 1935-36), and the pattern-burnishing is very much like that which begins in the Amuq B phase and goes on into C and even D, again in the same horizon. The very unusual "cheese pots" of Samos (Heidenreich, 1935-36, pp. 139-41, Pl. 34, 6)—wide flat dishes with an almost vertical rim and a row of holes pierced just below the lip, which occur at Cos and Calymnos, in Thessaly (Fig. 1, 13) and Macedonia, and one is said to have been found at Mallia in Crete—are also found at Ghassul (Mallon, Koeppel, and Neuville, 1934, p. 40, Pl. 51, 3). A most fascinating parallelism occurs in the Ghassul sherds with an overall pattern of impressed spirals (Fig. 1, 20) (Mallon, Koeppel, and Neuville, 1934, p. 120, Fig. 61, 5, 6, 8; Koeppel, 1940, p. 69, Pl. 86, 6), said to be made with small shells, which resemble remarkably the disconnected spirals on Cycladic frying pans (Fig. 1, 19) (Zschietzschmann, 1935, p. 661, Fig. 7) and which have never been considered in the vexing problem of the origin of spiraliform ornament in the Aegean. And in both places the typical burials show contracted skeletons in cist graves, while pithos or jar burials are also common to both and to early Troy. The multiplicity of similarities is further increased by material from other sites in

levels contemporary with Ghassul or possibly earlier. From Jericho VIII
there are grain pits or bothroi like those of Ghassul and the Aegean; the
double ones from Ghassul (Mallon, Koeppel, and Neuville, 1934, Pl. 21, 1)
are especially similar to those from Thermi (Lamb, 1936, p. 63, Pl. VII,
6). Jericho VIII also offers a system of construction using orthostates
(Garstang, 1935, pp. 163-64), or upright stones, bordering and protecting
the exterior of mud-brick walls; and the identical practice appears in the
lowest level of the Protesilas mound (Demangel, 1926, p. 16, Figs. 15-16),
contemporary with, or earlier than, the beginning of Troy I, as well as in
the second oldest stratum at Zerelia in Thessaly (Wace and Thompson,
1912, p. 161, Fig. 106), which is Middle Neolithic, and in Level M at Geoy
Tepe in Azerbaijan (Brown, 1951, p. 17), which Burton Brown equates with
northern Ubaid. Early dates are also suggested by the similarity of a very
special form of high tab handle which occurs in Mersin XIV (Goldman and
Garstang, 1947, p. 376, Fig. 4, 2-3) and again on Samos (Heidenreich, 1935-
36, Pl. 46, 4-5), where, unfortunately, the material is not stratified. The
combined evidence of all these similarities must cause the Aegean pre-
historian to hesitate about removing the earliest Cycladic material, the
sub-Neolithic of Crete and the Early Minoan I, the late Neolithic and Early
Helladic I of the mainland, earliest Troy I and the pre-Troy cultures of
Kum Tepe and Besika Tepe, as well as much of the material from Samos,
too far from the Ubaidian horizon of the Near East as manifest at Mersin,
in the Amuq, in Palestine, and even in Iran. The Syro-Cilician area is
again the most likely center of transmission. To return to my original
point, the early "Pelos" culture of the Cyclades is clearly older than
Bronze Age beginnings in either Crete or mainland Greece and may even
go back to the time of the Middle Neolithic period in these regions, which
may explain the lack thus far of a Neolithic assemblage in these islands.

The tripartite scheme for the Aegean Neolithic suggested five years
ago (Weinberg, 1947) has won general acceptance; but the place of the Late
Neolithic with respect to the beginning of the Early Bronze, with which I
believe it to be contemporary at least in part, has met with some objections
and some support. Nowhere is the stratification sufficiently clear in sites
excavated thus far to support fully either contention; excavation on a larger scale in pertinent strata is needed to decide the point. Nevertheless,
the Late Neolithic in Greece is known from abundant remains; the most
fully documented phase of it is the very specialized Thessalian Dimini culture. Much has been made of the spiraliform painted ornament on Dimini

pottery, which has usually been referred to the Bandkeramik of southeastern Europe; in fact, there seems to me to have been an overemphasis on
this one feature which has obscured others which are more important as
cultural traits. Especially so is the appearance at Dimini and Sesklo of a
very advanced architectural complex, comprising megaron and forecourt
within a fortified compound, usually with a gate opposite the megaron.
These features, formerly known in their most developed form in Troy II
and in the later Mycenaean palace, now already occur in the early phase
of Troy I. It has often been pointed out that Dimini stone figurines are
very similar to those of the Cyclades; more recently Miss Benton has
shown (1947, pp. 165-70) that many of the Dimini vase shapes are also
Cycladic, while others survive from the earlier Thessalian Neolithic,
along with a good part of the Dimini painted decoration. To the old designs have been added the spiral, rarely used in other than isolated examples inorganically dispersed among the older linear patterns. These,
too, may be Cycladic; and Kaschnitz-Weinberg has recently argued convincingly (Kaschnitz-Weinberg, 1949-50) that the Aegean spiral owes its
origin to Near Eastern metal-work with spiraliform wire decoration. Such
motifs could be derived from the Cyclades at a period earlier than Early
Helladic I, as we have just shown. The use of polychromy, while typical
of one class of Dimini ware, is equally characteristic elsewhere on the
mainland in the Late Neolithic, and there is good evidence to show that its
appearance in Greece precedes the Dimini culture; I believe it to be an
extension of the Jemdet Nasr polychromy. The Late Neolithic of the rest
of Greece, characterized by matt-painted pottery, polychrome ware, the
continuation of black-burnished pottery with rippled, pattern-burnished or
white-painted ornament, which began at the end of the Middle Neolithic,
and the continuation as well of the gray wares of the earlier phase, belongs
also in the Jemdet Nasr horizon, especially as manifest in Level XII at
Mersin, where there are also collected, though possibly in a telescoped
level, the survivors of Ubaid and Uruk periods, combined with Anatolian
black-burnished ware, often with white-painted patterns (Goldman and
Garstang, 1947, pp. 379-82). The Late Neolithic in Greece certainly parallels Jemdet Nasr in the Near East; it may begin earlier.

One of the elements of the Middle Neolithic of the Peloponnesus and
central Greece in particular, but known in Thessaly and Crete as well, is
the silvery-gray ware (Weinberg, 1937, pp. 503-11; 1947, p. 174, n. 71),
which in shape and fabric is but an extension of Uruk gray ware, such as

appeared in Levels XIV-XIII at Mersin. Though stratified deposits do not yet show this clearly, I believe the gray ware to be a late addition to the Middle Neolithic repertory, not one of its original characteristics. It indicates that the Middle Neolithic period ran into, if not through, the Uruk period; Late Neolithic may already have begun during this phase. Typical of the earlier phase of the Middle Neolithic is the glazed, or Neolithic Urfirnis, ware of the Peloponnesus and central Greece, which includes vases partly covered with dark-on-light painted designs in the same glaze, and the Thessalian red-slipped wares and painted pottery with similar shapes and designs. The glaze paint, the very angular metallic shapes of many of the bases, and many of the painted designs belong in the milieu of Halaf (Braidwood, 1952, Fig. 23), with strong similarities again to the somewhat provincial manifestations of this culture at Mersin. Some figurines decorated with glaze paint (Fig. 1, 21-22) (Holmberg, 1944, pp. 115-16, Fig. 111, 7-9, Pl. II, j-k; Weinberg, 1948, pp. 199-200, Pl. LXX, 1-2) have close parallels in Tall-i-Bakun A, in levels which McCown has equated with Ubaid, or possibly early Uruk (Fig. 1, 23) (Langsdorff and McCown, 1942, pp. 64-65, Pls. 6, 17; 7, 1, 4, 7-9). The more rounded shapes of the Chaeronea painted ware (Fig. 1, 24a-b) (Wace and Thompson, 1912, p. 198, Fig. 140a-e), transitional from Early to Middle Neolithic, have recently found striking parallels at Hassuna (Fig. 1, 25a-b) (Lloyd and Safar, 1945, Pls. XIV, 2, XV, XVI). The steatopygous figurines of clay also connect with Halafian (Oppenheim, 1943, Pl. 105) or earlier assemblages in the Near East (Braidwood, 1951, p. 992, Figs. 18 and 22; Lloyd and Safar, 1945, Pl. XVIII, 2), and they do not occur there later. There appears in central Greece and Thessaly, along with wares of the Middle Neolithic and perhaps earlier, a whole group of incised or impressed wares, some bearing incision combined with paint (Fig. 1, 26a) (Tsountas, 1908, Pls. 13-14), which belong to the Neolithic of Mersin (Goldman and Garstang, 1947, pp. 370-72, Fig. 1) and perhaps of Tarsus as well, to the pre-Halaf levels in the Amuq (Braidwood, 1952, Figs. 7-8) and at Sakce Gözü (Taylor, Seton-Williams, and Waechter, 1950, p. 90), to Hassuna (Fig. 1, 26b) (Lloyd and Safar, 1945, Figs. 13-14), and which seem to derive from an eastern Anatolian center.

With the Early Neolithic in Greece, best known in the northern Peloponnesus and in central Greece, we seem again to be in the time of Hassuna, the pre-Halaf of the Amuq, the Mersin Late Neolithic, in the time of the earliest appearance of painted pottery of hemispherical shapes, of

steatopygous female figurines, the first stamp seals, and the beveled celt.
For Crete, too, there are similarities with the pre-Halafian cultures, the
earliest Amuq phases, Megiddo XX.

If these parallelisms are based only on general similarities, they are
sufficiently numerous already to leave little doubt that the cultural sequence in the Aegean runs along exactly parallel with that of the Near
East, that each major phase in the latter region is reflected in the former
both in general and in particular; and, as more material is forthcoming
from the Aegean from stratified Neolithic sites, I am confident that the relationships will be drawn even closer. The Aegean was a province of the
Near East throughout its Neolithic phase and to a large extent during its
Early Bronze Age as well. There may have been some "cultural lag," but
not nearly as much as has often been adduced; much less is required now
that the dates of the respective cultures of the Near East have been drasti-
cally lowered. With the Aegean prehistoric phases firmly tied to those of
the eastern Mediterranean, their relative chronology is clear and their absolute dates wait upon the establishment of such in the Levant, where far
greater possibilities exist for accurate dating.

Table 1

The Relative Chronology of the Aegean and the Near East

Egypt	Connections	Crete	Cyclades	Greece	Troad	C. Anatolia	Cilicia	Mesopot.	Iran
Dyn. XII	Red-cross bowls ← - -	Middle Minoan	Middle Cycladic	Middle Helladic	Troy VI	Kültepe Phase Polatli	Middle Bronze Tarsus		
Dyn. XI & X	Eg. stamp impression - -			— x (Asine) Early Helladic III	Troy V	Levels 11-15 — x — End of EB	— x		Hissar IIIa — x Hissar IIb
Dyn. IX VIII VII	EM III & Eg. seal types	Early Minoan III	"Syros" Group — x		Troy IV / Troy III				
Dyn. VI	Double spiral pins, Gold jewelry & vessels	— x —			— x — Troy IIg	Alaca — x — Royal graves		Royal Tombs — x — at Ur	
Dyn. V	EM II stone vessels	Early Minoan II	Early Cycladic	Early Helladic II	Troy II				
Dyn. IV				Early Helladic	Troy I				

(Troad: ← Urfirnis imports — Early Helladic Early →)

100

Table 1 (continued)

Egypt	Connections	Crete	Cyclades	Greece	Troad	C. Anatolia	Cilicia	Mesopot.	Iran
Dyn. III	Megaron	Early Minoan I		Early Helladic I	Kum Tepe Ic Thermi	Alishar Copper Age		Jemdet Nasr	x Tall-i-Bakun A
Dyn. II & I	Bird-pins	Sub and Late	x	Late	x (Thermi I)				
	Black polished wares (pattern-burnishing)	Neolithic x	"Pelos" group	Neolithic (JN seal types) x	x Kum Tepe Ib Besika Tepe	Alishar Chalcolithic	x Mersin XII	x Uruk	x
	Gray ware	Middle	x	Middle	x		x Mersin XIV-XIII		
	"Urfirnis" figurines	Neolithic		Neolithic				Obeid	
	Steatopygous figs.	x Early Neolithic → ?	x	x Early Neolithic → ?	Kum Tepe IA(?)			x Halaf	
					Neolithic			Samarra Hassuna Neolithic	

101

Sources of Illustrations

1. Zygouries (Blegen, 1928, Fig. 69)

2. Asine (Frödin and Persson, 1938, Fig. 160, 2)

3. Brak (Mallowan, 1947, Pl. XXXII, 8)

4. Troy (Schliemann, 1880, p. 489, No. 836)

5. Alaca Höyük (Koşay, 1944, Pl. CIX, 26)

6. Troy (Schliemann, 1880, p. 489, No. 848)

7. Tepe Hissar (Schmidt, 1937, Pl. XXIX, H4856)

8. Syros (Tsountas, 1899, Pl. 10, 13)

9. Thermi (Lamb, 1936, Pl. XXV, 31.18)

10. Eutresis (Goldman, 1931, Pl. II)

11. Alishar Höyük (Schmidt, 1932, Pl. VII, b139)

12. Alishar Höyük (Von der Osten, 1937, Pl. VIII, b37)

13. Palaiokastro, Thessaly (B.C.H., 1932, p. 101, Fig. 11)

14. Cyclades (Weinberg, 1951, Pl. 2, A)

15. Crete (Weinberg, 1951, Pl. 1, A)

16. Amuq (Weinberg, 1951, Pl. 3, E)

17. Haghios Nikolaos, Crete (Evans, 1921-35, Vol. I, Fig. 24)

18. Ghassul (Mallon, Koeppel, and Neuville, 1934, Pl. 50, A)

19. Andros (Frankfort, 1927, Pl. VI, 4)

20. Ghassul (Mallon, Koeppel, and Neuville, 1934, Fig. 61, 6, 8)

21. Asea (Holmberg, 1944, Pl. II, k)

22. Corinth (Weinberg, 1948, Pl. LXXX, 2)

23. Tall-i-Bakun A (Langsdorff and McCown, 1948, Pl. 7, 4a)

24a-b. Chaeronea (Wace and Thompson, 1912, Fig. 140a and e)

25a-b. Tell Hassuna (Lloyd and Safar, 1945, Pls. XIV, 2, and XIII, 2)

26a. Argissa, Thessaly (Tsountas, 1908, Pl. 14, 4)

26b. Tell Hassuna (Lloyd and Safar, 1945, Fig. 14, 13)

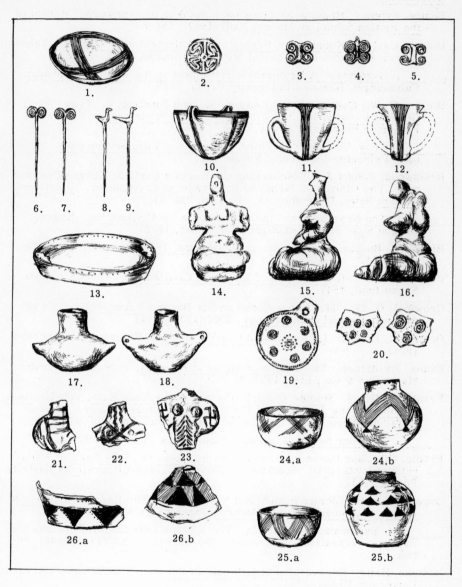

Fig. 1.—The Aegean and the Near East:
Some Comparative Traits

References

Benton, Sylvia. "Haghios Nikolaos near Astakos in Akarnania," Annual of the British School at Athens, XLII (1947), 156-83.

Blegen, Carl W. Korakou: A Prehistoric Settlement near Corinth. Boston: American School of Classical Studies at Athens, 1921.

_____. Zygouries: A Prehistoric Settlement in the Valley of Cleonae. Cambridge: Harvard University Press, 1928.

Blegen, C. W.; Caskey, J. L.; Rawson, M.; and Sperling, J. Troy, Vol. I: General Introduction, the First and Second Settlements. Princeton: Princeton University Press, 1950.

_____. Troy, Vol. II: The Third, Fourth, and Fifth Settlements. Princeton: Princeton University Press, 1951.

Braidwood, Robert J. "Discovering the World's Earliest Village Community: The Claims of Jarmo as the Cradle of Civilization," Illustrated London News, December 15, 1951, pp. 992-95.

_____. The Near East and the Foundations for Civilization. Eugene: Oregon State System of Higher Education, 1952.

Brown, T. Burton. Excavations in Azarbaijan, 1948. London: John Murray, 1951.

Childe, V. Gordon. The Dawn of European Civilization. 4th ed. London: Kegan Paul, 1947.

Crowfoot, G. M. "Mat Impressions on Pot Bases," Liverpool Annals of Archaeology and Anthropology, XXV (1938), 3-11.

Demangel, Robert. Le Tumulus dit de Protésilas. Paris: E. de Boccard, 1926.

Evans, Sir Arthur. The Palace of Minos at Knossos, Vols. I-IV. London: Macmillan & Co., Ltd., 1921-35.

Frankfort, Henri. Studies in Early Pottery of the Near East, Vol. II: Asia, Europe and the Aegean, and Their Earliest Interrelations. London: Royal Anthropological Institute of Great Britain and Ireland, 1927.

_____. Cylinder Seals. London: Macmillan & Co. Ltd., 1939.

Frödin, Otto, and Persson, Axel W. Asine: Results of the Swedish Excavations, 1922-1930. Stockholm: Generalstabens Litografiska Anstalts Förlag, 1938.

Garstang, John. "Jericho: City and Necropolis. Fifth Report," Liverpool Annals of Archaeology and Anthropology, XXII (1935), 143-88.

_____. "Explorations in Cilicia. The Neilson Expedition: Fifth Interim Report. Excavations at Mersin: 1938-39," ibid., XXVI (1939-40), 89-158.

Goldman, Hetty. Excavations at Eutresis in Boeotia. Cambridge: Harvard University Press, 1931.

_____. "Excavations at Gözlü Kule, Tarsus, 1938," American Journal of Archaeology, XLIV (1940), 60-86.

Goldman, Hetty, and Garstang, John. "A Conspectus of Early Cilician Pottery," American Journal of Archaeology, LI (1947), 370-88.

Heidenreich, Robert. "Vorgeschichtliches in der Stadt Samos. Die Funde," Athenische Mitteilungen, LX-LXI (1935-36), 125-83.

Heurtley, W. A, Prehistoric Macedonia. Cambridge: At the University Press, 1939.

Holmberg, Erik J. The Swedish Excavations at Asea in Arcadia. Lund: C. W. K. Gleerup, 1944.

Hutchinson, R. W. "Notes on Minoan Chronology," Antiquity, XXII (1948), 61-74.

Jirku, S. "Teleilat Ghassul und die Chronologie von Early Minoan I," Biblica, XXIX (1948), 269-71.

Kaschnitz-Weinberg, G. "Zur Herkunft der Spirale in der Agäis," Praehistorische Zeitschrift, XXXIV/V (1949-50), 193-215.

Koeppel, Robert. Teleilat Ghassul, Vol. II. Rome: Institut Biblique Pontifical, 1940.

Koşay, Hamit Zübeyr. Ausgrabungen von Alaca Höyük, 1936. ("Veröffentlichungen der türkischen Geschichtskommission," Ser. V, No. 2a.) Ankara, 1944.

_____. Les Fouilles d'Alaca Höyük, 1937-1939. ("Publications de la Société d'Histoire Turque.") Ankara, 1951.

Kunze, Emil. Orchomenos, Vol. III: Die Keramik der frühen Bronzezeit. Munich: Verlag der Bayerischen Akademie der Wissenschaften, 1934.

Lamb, Winifred. "Schliemann's Prehistoric Sites in the Troad," Praehistorische Zeitschrift, XXIII (1932), 111-31.

_____. Excavations at Thermi in Lesbos. Cambridge: At the University Press, 1936.

_____. "Excavations at Kusura near Afyon Karahisar. I," Archaeologia, LXXXVI (1936), 1-64.

_____. "Excavations at Kusura near Afyon Karahisar. II," ibid., LXXXVII (1938), 217-73.

Langsdorff, A., and McCown, D. E. Tall-i-Bakun A: Season of 1932. Chicago: University of Chicago Press, 1948.

Lemerle, Paul. "Chronique des fouilles et découvertes archéologiques en Grèce (1937)," Bulletin de correspondance hellénique, LXI (1937), 441-76.

Levi, Doro. "One of the Richest Finds of Minoan Treasures in Crete," Illustrated London News, January 19, 1952, pp. 106-8.

Lloyd, Seton, and Gökçe, Nuri. "Excavations at Polatli," Anatolian Studies, I (1951), 21-75.

Lloyd, Seton, and Safar, Fuad. "Tell Hassuna," Journal of Near Eastern Studies, IV (1945), 225-89.

Loud, Gordon. Megiddo, Vol. II: Seasons of 1935-39. Chicago: University of Chicago Press, 1948.

Mallowan, M. E. L. "Excavations at Brak and Chagar Bazar," Iraq, IX (1947), 1-266.

Mallon, A.; Koeppel, R.; and Neuville, R. Teleilat Ghassul, Vol. I. Rome: Pontificio Instituto Biblico, 1934.

Matz, Friedrich. Review in Gnomon, XVI (1940), 145-55.

_____. "Zur ägäischen Chronologie der frühen Bronzezeit," Historia, I (1950), 173-94.

Mylonas, George E. Excavations at Olynthus, Part I: The Neolithic Settlement. Baltimore: Johns Hopkins Press, 1929.

_____. "Excavations at Haghios Kosmas," American Journal of Archaeology, XXXVIII (1934), 258-79.

_____. "The Site of Akropotamos and the Neolithic Period in Macedonia," ibid., XLV (1941), 557-76.

Oppenheim, Max Freiherr von. Tell Halaf, Vol. I: Die praehistorischen Funde. Berlin: Walter de Gruyter & Co., 1943.

Osten, H. H. Von der. The Alishar Huyuk: Seasons of 1930-32, Part I. Chicago: University of Chicago Press, 1937.

Pendlebury, J. D. S. "Excavations in the Plain of Lasithi. I. The Cave of Trapeza," Annual of the British School at Athens, XXXVI (1935-36), 5-131.

_____. The Archaeology of Crete. London: Methuen & Co., Ltd., 1939.

Phylakopi. Excavations at Phylakopi in Melos. ("Society for the Promotion of Hellenic Studies, Supplementary Papers," No. 4.) London: Macmillan & Co., Ltd., 1904.

Schachermeyr, Fritz. "Die orientalisch-mittelmeerischen Grundlagen der vorgeschichtlichen Chronologie," Praehistorische Zeitschrift, XXXIV/V (1949-50), 17-48.

Schliemann, Heinrich. Ilios: The City and Country of the Trojans. New York: Harper & Bros., 1881.

Schmidt, Erich F. The Alishar Hüyük: Seasons of 1928 and 1929, Part I. Chicago: University of Chicago Press, 1932.

_____. Excavations at Tepe Hissar, Damghan. Philadelphia: University of Pennsylvania Press, 1937.

Seager, Richard B. Explorations in the Island of Mochlos. Boston: American School of Classical Studies at Athens, 1912.

Taylor, J. duPlat; Seton-Williams, M. V.; and Waechter, J. "The Excavations at Sakce Gözü," Iraq, XII (1950), 53-138.

Tsountas, Christos. "Kykladika II," Ephemeris archaiologike, 1899. Dimini and Sesklo. Athens: Sakellariou, 1908.

Valmin, M. Natan. The Swedish Messenia Expedition. Lund: G. W. K. Gleerup, 1938.

Wace, A. J. B., and Blegen, Carl W. "The Pre-Mycenaean Pottery of the Mainland," Annual of the British School at Athens, XXII (1918), 175-89.

Wace, A. J. B., and Thompson, M. S. Prehistoric Thessaly. Cambridge: At the University Press, 1912.

Weinberg, Saul S. "Remains from Prehistoric Corinth," Hesperia, VI (1937), 487-524.

_____. "Aegean Chronology: Neolithic Period and Early Bronze Age," American Journal of Archaeology, LI (1947), 165-82.

Weinberg, Saul S. "A Cross-section of Corinthian Antiquities (Excavations of 1940)," Hesperia, XVII (1948), 197-241.

_____, "Neolithic Figurines and Aegean Interrelations," American Journal of Archaeology, LV (1951), 121-33.

Woolley, Sir Leonard. Ur Excavations, Vol. II: The Royal Cemetery. Oxford: Oxford University Press, 1934.

_____. "On a Steatopygous Stone Figure from North Syria," Mélanges syriens offerts à Monsieur René Dussaud, pp. 135-37. Paris: P. Geuthner, 1939.

Zschietzschmann, W. "Kykladenpfannen," Archäologische Anzeiger, 1935, cols. 652-68.

The Relative Chronology of Southeastern and Central
Europe in the Neolithic Period

Robert W. Ehrich
Brooklyn College

General Considerations

When we come to the archeological sequences and chronological relationships of southeastern and central Europe, we enter a culture area
which is geographically set off from the Aegean and from Asia Minor.
There are several factors which make for difficulty in cross-dating the
cultures of this region with those of the south and east, and not the least
of them is the difficulty in correlating the sequences of its own subareas.

In cross-dating we are faced with the necessity of using materials
which are not only similar in any two areas but also firmly established as
to their cultural contexts, sufficiently limited in their time span that we
can consider them to be chronologically diagnostic, and sufficiently complex in character that we can treat them with some confidence as index
criteria. Because of the shadowy nature of much of the data, we are sometimes forced to violate some of these strictures.

Geographic, demographic, and ethnologic elements limit the range of
recognizable specific resemblances between established complexes. The
picture is further complicated by differentials in the degree of archeological exploitation, by political boundaries which cross-cut cultural entities,
by a welter of terminologies in different languages, and by orientations
which are sometimes colored by varying degrees of nationalism, parochi-
alism, or particular cultural theories on the part of the various inter-
preters.

As in the Aegean, Dr. Weinberg's dictum, that the reliability of a
specific chronology tends to vary in direct proportion to the age of an excavation, generally holds true, although some excavations of more recent
date have also been dug by questionable methods. To this, of course,
must be added the size of the sample, the degree of completeness of the
published data, and the actual selection of material for description and
illustration.

It must be remembered not only that in this region do we have the problem of cultural subareas but also that temperate Europe is a well-watered zone in which buildings were constructed of wood. This, when decomposed, tends to yield fewer architectural traces than do the stone and earth walls of the south and east and also results in much thinner occupation strata, which are consequently more difficult to excavate.

The situation is exacerbated by the semimigratory pattern of shifting agricultural settlements imposed by the available loess land and the techniques of hoe-culture (Childe, 1950, pp. 91-92; 1953, pp. 198-99). From the Neolithic period there seem to be relatively few sites which were continuously occupied for any length of time; and those which may be potentially revealing were usually excavated and published in such a manner as to obscure the actual developmental sequence.

In central Europe those sites which do show stratification are, for the most part, discontinuous and represent reoccupations following periods of abandonment. We are thus constantly faced with a question as to whether observable differences between the material of briefly inhabited sites or levels of the same complex represent time differences or whether they are merely local variations occurring between village units which are more or less contemporaneous. Much of the developmental sequence structure and cross-datings within the area have been painstakingly erected by cross-analysis from site to site with relatively little actual stratigraphy from which to draw. The nature of the terrain, moreover, renders extremely difficult any consideration of the time lag necessary for diffusion.

The Geographic Framework

A rapid survey of the geographical situation gives the following results. The two subareas lying closest to Anatolia and the Aegean are the Lower and Middle Danube basins, which are separated from each other by the rugged mountainous strip which runs from Golubac to Turnu Severin, the terminus of the Iron Gate. Macedonia, I think, has been erroneously interpreted, first as part of a corridor marked by a through route along the Vardar and Morava rivers (Hawkes, 1940, pp. 94-95, 106-9; Childe, 1947, pp. 80 ff.; 1950, p. 50; Gaul, 1948, p. 86), and more recently as an extension of a Vardar-Morava culture (Childe, 1947, pp. 86-90). Actually, many elements of the so-called "Vardar-Morava culture," which might also be described as Middle Danubian Middle Neolithic, do not seem to have penetrated very far down the Vardar as a complex. Throughout its history, Macedonia seems rather to have been a transition zone in which elements from the north, south, and east were fused into distinctively local complexes, the details of which are still not clear cut (Heurtley, 1939; Weinberg, 1951, p. 407).

As far as can be ascertained, the Neolithic of western Bulgaria seems to belong to the Middle Danubian sphere. Gaul's survey of this area (1948) was based almost entirely on surface collections; and, although western elements are certainly dominant, actual sequential assemblages have not been defined. The Neolithic of eastern Bulgaria occurs in tells, ties in well with the Wallachian sequence of southern Rumania, and forms a part of the related East European Painted Band-Ceramics groups which cover the Ukraine, Bukovina, Moldavia, and Transylvania. The Marica Valley opens to the south, and, for the early period at least, it must be considered as a part of the Aegean area.

On the Middle Danube the situation is also difficult. The site of Vinča, which stands alone in affording a deep deposit representing continuous occupation, was dug by arbitrary 10-cm. levels (Fewkes, 1936, pp. 20 ff.; Milojčić, 1949b, p. 259), and the material was grouped accordingly, without reference to the original cultural assemblages. Irregularities in the ground level, intrusions, and disturbances were thus ignored, and it is consequently impossible to establish satisfactorily an assemblage of associated material for any given period complex. Holste (1939) has made a valiant attempt to determine the developmental sequence, but the outlines remain blurred. Instead of serving as the key to the region, as it properly should, the history of Vinča is gradually being unraveled by reference to other sites. Farther west on the Drave, the site of Sarvaš has been tested, and the brief discussion concerning it is suggestive and tantalizing (Schmidt, 1945, pp. 127-31).

On the Hungarian plain the Danube serves as something of a barrier between its eastern (or Tisza, followed by Bodrogkeresztur) and its western (or Linear, followed by Lengyel and finally by Baden) culture groups (Childe, 1929, pp. 76 ff.; 1947, pp. 101 ff.; Tompa, 1937, pp. 40 ff.). The Moravian Corridor, which separates the Carpathians from the plateau of Bohemia, opens from the western Hungarian plain or Little Alföld and leads northward. Thus the Lengyel group of western Hungary has a clearly related extension in the Moravian Painted group (Childe, 1929, pp. 82 ff.) and an outlier in the Jordansmühl complex of Silesia (Seger, 1926; Schránil, 1927-28, pp. 50 ff., 55 ff.; Stocký, 1929, pp. 80-88).

The northern (or western) Carpathians of Slovakia pretty well delimit the area with which we have to deal. In strictly geographical terms, Bohemia, which in its entirety comprises the drainage of the northward-flowing upper Elbe rather than a part of the Danube Basin, would normally be left out of account. Archeologically, however, the cultural sequences of Bohemia have been well worked out, and, because of its intermediate position, this region throws valuable light on the relationships between the sequences of the surrounding areas (Schránil, 1927-28; Stocký, 1929).

This, then, is the geographical frame of our materials. The Middle-Danubian and Bohemian subareas will serve as our point of departure.

The Starčevo-Körös Complex

In the Middle Danube Basin, then, the oldest recognizable Neolithic deposits seem to be those of the Starčevo-Körös group (Fewkes, Goldman, and Ehrich, 1933, pp. 48 ff.; Fewkes, 1936, p. 77; Tompa, 1937, p. 46; Hawkes, 1940; Kutzian, 1944, 1947; Childe, 1947, pp. 86 ff.; Milojčić, 1949a, pp. 70-72; 1949b), although at the site of Oszentiván VIII there is some evidence for at least a partial, if not complete, overlap with Vinča A (Banner and Parducz, 1948, pp. 36, 39 ff.). These sites are numerous and cover a large area along the Tisza, Körös, and the Danube but are, so far, only incompletely known. Their distribution stretches from western Bulgaria, where Gaul (1948, p. 21) has recognized Starčevo-Körös traits, westward at least as far as Sarvaš on the Drave (Schmidt, 1945, pp. 127-31). Attempts to cross-date them have been confused by several factors. Childe (1947, pp. 334-36) has argued reasonably for a relatively short chronology; and Schmidt's results at Sarvaš also point in this direction (see also Fewkes, 1936, pp. 76-77). Milojčić (1949a, p. 69 and end-table), however, places this culture well back in the second half of the fourth millennium.

The complex is found as an entity in some sites unmixed with the obviously later incised and painted band-ceramics, which do not occur at Starčevo or in some of the Körös sites but which do overlie it at Vinča (Fewkes, 1936, pp. 27 ff.; Childe, 1947, pp. 86-89) and apparently at Tordos (Roska, 1936). In general, the character of each settlement indicates a rather short period of habitation, and the pattern of shifting hoe-culture suggests that any recognizable time differences would appear primarily between different sites occupied by the same groups of people.

On stylistic grounds an attempt has been made to divide this culture into four stages (Milojčić, 1949b, pp. 261-66). As a whole, the pottery complex of the Körös culture comprises a plain ware with rough finger

ornamentation and a smeared clay coating called "rusticated" or "barbotine" which is radically different from the so-called "barbotine" wares of
Crete and the Aegean (Fig. 1). A few forms of this group show strong resemblances to some of those of Thessalian A. Also appearing on some of
the larger vessels is the crude plastic representation of animal and human forms. However, at Starčevo (Fewkes, Goldman, and Ehrich, 1933,
pp. 43, 45), at Bubanj on the Morava (Orssich-Slavetich, 1940, pp. 26 ff.),
at Sarvaš (Schmidt, 1945, pp. 127-31), and some other sites, pottery with
black paint on a red-burnished slip characteristic of Dimini or Thessalian
B (Fig. 2) is associated with Körös-type plain ware of Sesklo affinities
(cf. Wace and Thompson, 1912). Typical Dimini shapes are lacking, but
the use of curvilinear and spiral motifs, often combined with rectilinear
geometric ones, is highly indicative. There are also some patterns characteristic of Thessalian A but rendered in Thessalian B technique.

The sampling is insufficient, but there may be some cleavage between
sites which show the presence of painted wares and those which do not.
Chronological interpretations are at least partly hinged on flat and unsub-
stantiated statements by Fewkes (1936, pp. 27, n. 109, 33, 73, n. 491, 77;
1937, p. 391) that at Starčevo unpainted wares occur earlier than do the
painted. Fewkes made these statements subsequent to the publication of
our joint preliminary report, in which we indicated clearly that the characteristic painted ware appeared in all the earliest deposits, including the
pits dug into the virgin soil, their associated wells, and in the debris lying
directly upon virgin soil (Fewkes, Goldman, and Ehrich, 1948, pp. 38 ff.).
I have rechecked our notes and our field catalogue of material and have
consulted with other members of the expedition. I can find no basis what-
soever for any stratigraphic indication that the first appearance of painted
wares at Starčevo is any later than the period of original settlement.

At Tordos on the Maros, unpainted wares are also reported as preceding painted (Childe, 1947, p. 89). Here, however, the painted wares over-
whelmingly belong to the later Band-Ceramic period, and we must have
at least two distinct Neolithic phases. Whether the rather scanty Starčevo
painted is really separated from an unpainted Körös complex is far from
clear. Generally it would seem that the painted wares are probably present but rare in the earlier part of the Starčevo-Körös period. Up to now,
however, with the possible exception of Sarvaš, there is no stratigraphic
indication of any priority for unpainted pottery of the Körös type.

We have, then, close resemblances in the Sesklo shapes of the plain ware, legged lamps or altars, flat bone spoons, Thessalian-type figurines, and the like, which make up a complex that is marked here and there by a Dimini ware painted in Dimini motifs. We must also stress not only that many Sesklo and Dimini types are lacking but also that, in Thessaly and Macedonia, early Neolithic shapes and wares seem to have survived into the later period. In terms of cultural dynamics and probabilities, it is difficult to accept the concept of two waves of migration of peoples with almost identical cultures, in which the main difference is only in a very restricted series of ceramic features, for their roots would lie in highly complex associations in each of the two parent-cultures. It may be further questioned as to how far this painted ware is likely to represent a later diffusion of a very limited ceramic character, in which close relationship is discernible but in which other striking details which were originally associated, such as shape and other styles of painting, did not spread with it. On these grounds, then, it seems impossible at the present time to equate an unpainted phase of the Starčevo-Körös complex with Sesklo and a later painted one with Dimini. It looks more as though some groups of a peripheral people with an essentially Sesklo or Thessalian A body of pottery adopted some Thessalian B ceramic traits before migrating into the area. It would thus seem that the Starčevo-Körös group cannot be correlated chronologically with anything in the Aegean that precedes Thessalian B.

The site of Sarvaš, near Osiek on the Drave (Schmidt, 1945, pp. 127-31), has so far been only mentioned but may throw some light on this question. We have as yet no clear statement concerning the adequacy of the sample from the lower levels, and the description is in terms of depths rather than of assemblages from specific units. As in Vinča, irregularities of the ground may vitiate some of the results, and we must await a final publication.

With these cautions in mind, we start a rough stratification with Level Ia consisting of Neolithic pit dwellings and unpainted pottery, which is inadequately described and which may be Starčevo-Körös in type but which does not sound like it. The depths of this level are given as 8.20-7.40 meters. Level Ib lies between 7.40 and 4.90 meters and is a thick deposit containing a variety of wares which suggest a further stratification. Taken by depth alone, a completely unreliable procedure, we find urfirnis ware at 6.80 meters; Late Linear ware with dot-filled bands at 6.50 meters; perforated pedestals like the western Hungarian Lengyel at 6.20 meters; geometric Starčevo painted at 6.00 meters; spiral-decorated at 5.80 meters; a Körös-type human plastic figure on a sherd at 5.60 meters; and fine cannelated and late Bükk wares at 5.40 meters. In this stratum we probably have an underlying Starčevo level, some contents of which were continuously thrown up by disturbance during later occupations.

The presence of urfirnis ware early in Level Ib, if not due to an intrusion, gives us a further clue. Although Milojčić (1949a, pp. 82 ff.) calls this ware "Greek Middle Neolithic," Weinberg (1951, p. 408) has demonstrated that this is an impossible identification. It is of interest that Schmidt, the excavator (1945, pp. 127-31), has definitely labeled it "Early Helladic," and this does seem to fit the picture. Whether or not it actually occurs early in Ib, this ware still has considerable significance. Allowing for time lag in diffusion, it cannot be much earlier than Early Helladic II and may be even later. Since Thessalian B overlaps at least Early Helladic I (Weinberg, 1947, pp. 172 ff.), there should be ample time to allow for the equation of the Starčevo-Körös complex with Thessalian B.

In the discussion that followed the reading of this paper at the symposium, Dr. Weinberg further pointed out that the typical Starčevo-Körös barbotine ware, which is foreign to Greece, appears in a lower level of the Protesilas mound and thus furnishes a further chronological correlation with Troy I (Demangel, 1926, not seen; Weinberg, 1947, p. 173).

The Incised Linear-Volute-Bükk-Zseliz Complex

For Bohemia and Moravia, Milojčić (1949a, end-table) has again put the oldest Neolithic wares with simple forms and incised volute decoration back into the fourth millennium. However, this ware is clearly related to the more elaborately incised Bükk ceramics of northern Hungary and Slovakia (Fig. 3), which have been found in the Bihor-Oradea area mixed with crusted painting (Nestor, 1933, p. 53). On the Hungarian plain Bükk is demonstrably younger than the Starčevo-Körös complex (Kutzian, 1947, pp. 33, 41-44). Furthermore, in addition to the incised spirals and volutes, there are some vessels occurring toward the end of Bohemian Ia which are ornamented by bands of spirals in crusted paint over an incised decoration of the transitional Šarka type (Fig. 3) (Jira, 1911; Schránil, 1927, p. 42; Stocký, 1929, p. 58). In Bohemia, Phases Ia and Ib both seem to have been of short duration, and the cross-ties of the later Bohemian cultures of Childe's Period III are demonstrably so late that, unless the dating of Period I is brought down, there is a considerable gap which is not adequately filled by the scanty Jordansmühl remains. The use of incision in both the Volute and the Bükk wares strongly suggests a post-Körös chronological position, and the curvilinear patterns seem to equate them with Holste's Vinča C, perhaps starting with Vinča B2 at the earliest. Further cross-finds would seem to confirm the following equation:

Bohemian Volute = west Hungarian Linear = Tisza I = Bükk I - Vinča B-C.

It must be stressed that essentially these groups are geographically distinct, and one must postulate that the mountainous area of northern Hungary and Slovakia, as well as the Bohemian plateau, must be regarded as peripheral regions settled somewhat later than the Middle Danubian plains.

At Nieswiska in the loess lands of Poland, Nestor (1933, p. 42, n. 139) notes that Tripolye A—Cucuteni A painted ware was associated with linear ceramics with at least one occurrence of the music-note type. In Moravia the music-note is not found in the earliest phase of the painted sequence (Childe, 1929, p. 38), and in the Gran Valley of Slovakia, the music-note is again associated with crusted painting at Zseliz (Nestor, 1933). Wilke (1929) describes the Zseliz pottery as linear ware with traces of paint, related to the Šarka type found at the end of the Volute phase (Childe's Ia) in Bohemia. In Hungary, Zseliz ware is pretty well limited to the northwestern part of the country. Tompa, in turn, considers linear ware to be the oldest in western Hungary (1937, p. 28), closely allied to Phases Ia and Ib in Bohemia (p. 30), and sees Tisza influences in late linear. From Nagytétény he reports (p. 32) a grave with typical music-note pottery of the Zseliz type that also contained an imported Bükk II vessel.

Actual durations are unknown, and the precise relationship of the linear wares of western Hungary with the Tisza wares of the east are not yet clear. However, from along the Tisza, Childe (1929, pp. 61 and Fig. 55) figures Bükk "negative-style" painting on a Danubian II bottle shape from Tisza Dob. Another cross-tie is the occurrence of a bowl decorated in Bükk "negative style" on a hut floor at Marosvasarhely on the upper Maros, where it was associated with the characteristic Ariuşd wares of Transylvania (Childe, 1929, p. 104). Childe further reports Band-Ceramic sherds as occurring in the A stratum at Cucuteni (1923, p. 265).

The Bükk culture was apparently of long duration and has been tentatively subdivided into three phases, more on stylistic grounds and associations than on the basis of actual stratification (Tompa, 1929, pp. 28-37). At Oros in Szabolcs County, Korek (1951) reports pottery of Bükk II-III styles as found with dishes characteristic of the southern Tisza region.

However, in two pits late Bükk ware occurred in association with Aeneolithic pottery with no apparent signs of disturbance. If this is correct, it
would indicate a late survival of Bükk III. Korek also quotes Csalog to
the effect that at Niyerseg, Bükk, and Tisza elements were mixed. The
equations summarizing this evidence would thus seem to be

Bükk II = Zseliz = Šarka (terminal Bohemian Ia); and
Bükk II-III = Bohemian Ib = Tisza late I and II = Ariuşd = Cucuteni A.

Since Tisza imports are known from the Vinča Middle levels at 3.8
and 5.5 meters and also with early Stroked or Danubian Ib in Silesia (Buttler, 1938a, pp. 29-30), Bükk III should equate with Vinča D and Lengyel-
Jordansmühl, while Bükk I should correlate as follows:

Bükk I = Tisza I ? = west Hungarian Linear = Bohemian Volute (Ia)
= Vinča B-C = Boian A.

Vinča: the Middle Levels

Returning now to the area of the middle Danube, we must have recourse to the admittedly shaky evidence from Vinča. Holste (1939), in
attempting to break down the post-Starčevo-Körös deposits into rough
period assemblages, has assigned them letter designations. Vinča A-C
represents a fairly long period, apparently marked by internal phasal development as well as by outside influences. These phases cannot at present be sharply distinguished (Milojčić, 1949a, p. 72). Holste's A and B
phases (1939, pp. 2-4) contain dot-filled incised bands with angular design, while, according to him, curvilinear patterns and true spirals as
well as face lids begin in Vinča C. Milojčić (1949b, pp. 274-78), however,
assigns the first appearance of both the curvilinear dot-filled incised ribbons and the face lids to Vinča B. Childe also describes them as present
but rare in the deeper levels. Owing to the manner of excavation and description, it is, of course, impossible to tell whether or not their sparse
occurrence represents a true early appearance or is merely the result
of intrusions from later periods. Both features occur most commonly in
Vinča C. Although not identical (Fig. 4), face lids first appear at Troy toward the end of Troy II and are mostly found in Troy III-V (Blegen et al.,
1950, p. 236; 1951, p. 31).

Milojčić (1949a, p. 72) is probably correct in his rejection of Holste's
Vinča A as contemporary with the Starčevo level at Vinča (however, see
Banner and Parducz, 1948, for some evidences of what may be at least a

partial contemporaneity). If we tentatively accept the rest of Holste's analysis, we get an interesting result. At Tarsus in Cilicia (personal information kindly supplied by Miss Goldman; see also her paper in this volume, pp. 71-72 n.) in Early Bronze Age II there is a welter of incised pottery of differing but associated styles. Of these, one group is decorated with incised, parallel, dot-filled bands, some of which have distinctly curvilinear patterns. One vessel has such a band wrapped spirally around it, but the true spiral of Danubian type seems to be absent. The olive-shaped pitcher with high, thin neck on which this ribboning occurs is not found on the Danube. This type of decoration, however, is associated with slipped and burnished wares and is strongly reminiscent of the band-ceramics of the Middle Danube which at Vinča may begin with Vinča B and are common in Vinča C and D (Fig. 5; and see Miss Goldman's Fig. 1, a_1, p. 82). Since Miss Goldman puts the end of Early Bronze II at Tarsus somewhere from Troy IId to IIg and begins her Early Bronze III somewhat before the beginning of Troy III, we may have another peg for our equation that Vinča C-D overlaps Troy IIg and Troy III.

On the basis of incised curvilinear patterns, Holste (1939, p. 11) implies a chronological relationship between the late Bükk ceramics of northern Hungary and Vinča C. Since we have already equated this with the Tisza I complex through crusted painting, it is not surprising to find late Tisza wares appearing in his Vinča D (ibid., p. 12).

"Period III": Late Neolithic-Aeneolithic

With Vinča E we enter the late Neolithic or Aeneolithic, which Childe (1929, pp. 112 ff.) terms "Danubian III." This is a period of expansion, and local groups came into frequent contact. The central and southeastern European cultures abound in cross-ties and indirectly provide further anchor points with the Aegean. Period III is followed by a transitional phase known as "Toszeg A" in Hungary (Tompa, 1937, p. 65), "Pre-Unětice" or "Pre-Aunjetitz" in Bohemia (Schránil, 1927-28, pp. 86-90), and "Marschwitz" in Silesia (Childe, 1929, p. 223; Seger, 1927), in which the various elements of the different Period III groups become fused to form the subsequent Early Bronze Age of middle Europe. The survivals from late local Neolithic and Aeneolithic cultures are clearly traceable, and the end-products show regional variations partly in accordance with the different emphasis and patternings of the older groups. This stage of fusion demonstrates the contemporaneity of the component elements at least at the end of Period III.

During Period II a regional variant of the painted Lengyel ceramics of western Hungary appeared in the Moravian corridor, which, in turn, leads northward into Silesia and the Sudeten lands. There a further extension of this tradition, clearly recognizable despite the loss of painted decoration, is known as "Jordansmühl" (Seger, 1926; Schránil, 1927, pp. 55 ff.; Stocký, 1929, pp. 80-88). At the type site, although most of the assemblages contained material characteristic of the Jordansmühl complex alone, a few contained associations of Jordansmühl types with Danubian I wares and others with the Danordic Baden group of Period III (Childe, 1929, p. 90). On the strength of the metal objects found in the graves, Buttler (1938b, p. 43) has correlated the Jordansmühl culture with that of the Hungarian Copper Age of Puszta-Istvanháza.

In Bohemia some Jordansmühl sherds have been found together with stroked ware of terminal Danubian Ib (Stocký, 1929, p. 87); and a few later unmixed deposits intervene before the onset of Period III (Schránil, 1927, pp. 5-9; Stocký, 1929, pp. 88 ff.). Some Jordansmühl elements, moreover, form a component of the early Danordic (Böhm, 1942, p. 61; also personal communication from Dr. Böhm and visible in the earlier phase of Homolka, unpublished), which is one of a series of Period III groups now blanketed under the name of "Baden" (Childe, 1947, pp. 112-14).

Although beyond the scope of this paper, it should be mentioned that Buttler (1938b, pp. 38 ff.) has used both Tisza and Jordansmühl traits as important criteria for documenting the chronological position of some of the central and southern German groups.

In Bohemia, then, Period III seems to begin with an influx of Jordansmühl and Jordansmühl elements from Silesia, the Sudeten lands, and Moravia. During the course of Period III there is a penetration southward from the northern European plain of various groups of people who had stone battle-axes and cord-impressed pottery of different styles marked by collar flasks, funnel beakers, globular amphorae, and the like. At approximately the same time the Saxo-Thuringian Corded Beaker people, also with battle-axes, expanded eastward. The close of the period is marked by the entry of the Bell Beaker people, after which the fusion into Pre-Unĕtice took place. In the middle Danube Basin a similar expansion penetrated the already settled area west of the Danube (Mozsolics, 1942b, p. 38), but corded ware and battle-axes are only found blended with Baden and Bell Beaker cultural contexts. Along the Drave the Baden culture appears earlier than the characteristic Late Slavonian at Vučedol

(Schmidt, 1945, Fig. 4, pp. 8, 140 ff.) and Sarvaš (ibid., p. 129); but at
Zók in southern Hungary the two are reported as contemporaneous (Tompa,
1937, p. 61). The Vučedol type of Late Slavonian has also been demonstrated as contemporaneous with that of the Bell Beaker people in northern and northwestern Hungary and in Lower Austria (Kastner, 1939; Willvonseder, 1939); and corded ware has been linked with both bell beakers
(Mozsolics, 1942b, pp. 41 f.) and with Laibach and Vučedol wares (ibid.,
pp. 43 f.). Bell Beaker and Baden remains, furthermore, have been
equated in Transdanubia or western Hungary (Mozsolics, 1942a, p. 87).

The significance of this situation lies in the fact that certain pottery
types, such as the cross-footed bowl (Fig. 6), typical of the Slavonian
wares (Childe, 1929, pp. 209, 211, 213), occur in the later part of the Danordic Baden group in Bohemia (Childe, 1929, p. 120; Stocký, 1929, p. 134;
Fewkes, 1932, p. 380), and the Danordic, in turn, is equated with the Hungarian Baden (Tompa, 1937, pp. 48 ff.). Since this is the period in which
corded ware penetrates middle and southeastern Europe, the specific occurrence of a cord-impressed sherd at the end of Early Helladic III at
Eutresis (Goldman, 1931, p. 123) helps to pin this period down. Childe,
furthermore (1940, pp. 174-75, Fig. 136), has recently emphasized the
close correspondence between the Slavonic cross-footed bowls and the
lamps from the Catacomb graves of the Manych and the Kuban.

There is, however, a rather puzzling situation with regard to Vinča
D and E. Milojčić (1949b, p. 299) correlates the Baden complex with the
transition from the Early to the Middle Aegean Bronze Age; and, since
this seems to equate through its contemporaneity with corded ware with
the end of Early Helladic III at Eutresis, his assignment seems valid.
However, for Vinča D he notes that the cross is frequently used as a motif of polished decoration on the inside of bowls. For Troy V, Blegen
et al. (1951, pp. 227 ff., 249 ff., Figs. 240, 246, etc.) describe the decoration of some of the red-cross bowls as executed in a burnished-red slip.
Weinberg (see his paper, this volume, pp. 89-90, and his Fig. 1) has discussed this trait as diagnostic of the close of the Early Bronze Age over
a wide area. At Vinča, then, we would expect to find them associated with
Baden remains rather than preceding them.

At present there would seem to be three possible explanations: (1)
The Baden-Corded Ware-Vučedol-Bell Beaker phase might be of much
briefer duration than Troy V, to which Blegen (1951, p. 230) has assigned
a span of 100-150 years. At the two-period Baden site of Homolka in

Bohemia (final publication in preparation) the total length of occupation seems to have been considerably less than a century and perhaps not more than 50 years. Corded and Bell Beaker wares, furthermore, seem to have survived somewhat later as separate entities during the formative stage of the Early Bronze Age than did those of Baden (Patay, 1937, pp. 45 ff.; Pittioni, 1941, pp. 49-51). If this is the case, the latter part of Vinča D would correlate with the early part of Troy V. (2) At Vinča the red-cross bowls may actually belong to the Baden assemblage of Vinča E, and this may be still another case in which the true relationships within the Vinča stratification have been confused by the manner of excavation. (3) In this instance we may not be dealing with a true parallel, and the Vinča material may not be comparable to that of Troy (Fig. 7). Those figured by Vasić (1936a, Pl. XCVI, 362; and 1936b, Pl. XLII, 103, e.g., Pl. LXIV, 1796) are on bowls of Danubian rather than Mediterranean and Aegean shapes and only Figure 362 shows the true cross. However, the technique as described is suggestive. All the Vinča examples came from depths listed as from 2 to 4 meters.

The Lower Danube

In the lower Danube Basin the situation seems even less clear-cut than along the middle Danube. In the eastern part of Bulgaria is a series of sites which stratigraphically presents the same sequence as that found on the Rumanian side (Gaul, 1948, pp. 64 ff., 86 ff.). Of these, Boian A is characterized by excised wares. This, in turn, is followed by the Bulgarian Mound Culture, essentially the same as the Rumanian Gumelnitza, which is marked by the liberal use of graphite paint. Above the culture levels of this period have been found some traces of cord-marked ware in the Oltenian Schneckenberg strata, which correlate with Glina III in Wallachia.

As to how this sequence ties up with that of the middle Danube, opinions vary. Milojčić (1949a, p. 64 and end-table) equates Boian A with the later phases of Starčevo and Vinča A; Gaul (1948, p. 233) with Vinča B; and Holste (1939, pp. 12, 13, 21) with Vinča C. In addition to the occurrence of a Middle Danube type of socketed ladle (Childe, 1929, pp. 77, 85, 91, Fig. 40) (Fig. 8) in the brief late Boian A "transition" level of Vidra II (Gaul, 1948, pp. 69, 76), a Wallachian-type peg-footed bowl (Fig. 9) found at Kökénydomb (Banner, 1930, Pl. XXXI, 2) apparently cross-dates this complex to a context in which Tisza II sherds were reported as associated with the characteristic dot-filled bands of the Middle Vinča levels (Childe, 1937, p. 486; Gaul, 1948, p. 76). It seems probable, then, that Boian A falls in the Vinča Middle levels and overlaps B and C. Buttler (1938a, p. 31) also cites an apparent Boian A import in what seem to be the Vinča Middle levels.

Be that as it may, the stratigraphically younger Gumelnitza-Bulgarian Mound Culture has yielded askoi (Fig. 10) which are characteristic of Early Helladic II and III (Gaul, 1948, pp. 85, 89, 99, 105), and this complex can apparently be equated with Ariuşd in Transylvania and Cucuteni A in Moldavia (Gaul, 1948, p. 108). Late Ariuşd pottery, in turn, has been found in association with Bodrogkeresztur wares (Childe, 1947, p. 136), which represent Period III of the Tisza culture; and these cross-date to Vinča E. In addition, Holste (1939, p. 18) cites an askos from Salcutza in a context which he equates with Vinča D. The Mound Culture itself seems to have been of long duration, while the overlying Glina III phase seems to have been quite brief and apparently cross-ties through the Schneckenberg Corded and Vadastra "A" to the end of Early Helladic III at Eutresis (Goldman, 1931, p. 123; Gaul, 1948, p. 215). Holste (1939, pp. 19, 20) thinks it possible to distinguish earlier and later askoi, with the younger group coming from the post-Gumelnitza levels of Schneckenberg. If he is correct, this would cross-date the Glina III—Schneckenberg Corded levels to Early Helladic III and equate Gumelnitza and the Mound Culture with Early Helladic II and perhaps the early part of III.

Gaul (1948, pp. 213 ff.), furthermore, agrees with Nestor (1933, pp. 56-57) that the Vadastra "B" culture, which occurred beneath levels containing Glina III corded ware in Wallachia and eastern Bulgaria, is contemporary with the Mound Culture. He also calls attention to the striking similarity between the Vadastra "B" white-filled, coarsely excised wares (Nestor, 1933, Pl. V, 11) and those of Phthiotic Thebes, which were said to overlie Dimini wares and which thus may well belong to Thessalian III (Wace and Thompson, 1912, pp. 166-68, Fig. 113) (Fig. 14).

Macedonian Connections

At Bubanj near Niš on the Morava, the later strata show a northward drift of Macedonian elements. Bubanj II represents a discontinuity with the preceding Stratum I or Starčevo-Körös level. Combined graphite and crusted painting typical of the Černavoda aspect of the Mound Culture have been found both in Bubanj II and at Ariuşd (Orssich-Slavetich, 1940, p. 29

ff.; Gaul, 1948, p. 100), thus cross-tying this level. Childe (1947, pp. 90-91) notes that this graphite-crusted combination was found with tankards and cups (Fig. 11) like those of the Macedonian Early Bronze Age.

Gaul (1948, p. 105) calls attention to typical Mound Culture–Gumelnitza graphite painted sherds from Vardina (Heurtley, 1939, p. 71) and Olynthus (Mylonas, 1929, p. 50), where they were found in Macedonian Late Neolithic contexts. Since in Bulgaria and Rumania this ware is found with askoi typical of Aegean Early Bronze Age inspiration, this would argue further in support of Weinberg's (1947, pp. 171-74) overlapping of northern Greek and Macedonian Neolithic with the Early Helladic farther south. Heurtley (1939, pp. 128 ff.) also argues for such an overlap. Since we have already equated the Starčevo-Körös complex with Thessalian B, it would seem that the Late Neolithic of Macedonia probably survived later than did that of Thessaly; spanned that of Boian A, which does not seem to have been of long duration; and lasted well into the Gumelnitza-Mound Culture period.

In the Late Neolithic II and III levels of Olynthus, Mylonas (1929, p. 50, Fig. 66) found black-on-red sherds very like those from Starčevo and Dimini (Fig. 2), and a vessel fragment (Fig. 12) with decoration very much in the Tisza style (Mylonas, 1929, Fig. 59; Childe, 1947, p. 105). This last may well belong to Late Neolithic III. A weaker parallel is the fragment (Fig. 13) of a zoömorphic vase from Olynthus (Mylonas, 1929, pp. 25 ff., Figs. 35, 36; Heurtley, 1939, p. 76, Fig. 160), possible relatives of which Böhm (1942, pp. 45 ff.) assigns to the end of Danubian II and as a carry-over into the early Aeneolithic of Period III. Perhaps somewhat more convincing are Heurtley's sketches (1939, p. 120) of Lengyel forms which he considers very close parallels to the Macedonian Early Bronze Age. At Vardina, Heurtley (1939, p. 35) reports no Early Bronze Age stratum, but he did find Late Neolithic and Early Bronze Age wares together. It is possible, of course, that the soundings at Vardina may have missed an Early Bronze Age level present elsewhere on the site.

I have deliberately omitted a detailed treatment of Macedonia from this discussion, for at present its sequences do not seem too firmly established or sufficiently fleshed out. The Danubian traits cited by Heurtley (1939, pp. 114 ff.) are such that it is difficult to localize them in time and place, although, as he points out, several seem at home along the Tisza. It would be a mistake, I think, to regard them as representing a northern complex or as an extension of a specific Danubian culture. They seem rather to be Danubian elements which diffused more or less independently and were absorbed and fused into a strong local cultural tradition.

Considering the age and character of the Macedonian samples, the following tentative correlations are admittedly shaky.

Olynthus Late Neolithic II-III overlaps Starčevo and Dimini and extends well into Danubian II, into Early Gumelnitza, and into the early part of the Bulgarian Mound Culture.

Macedonian Early Bronze Age = Late Lengyel in Hungary = Bubanj II = the later part of the Gumelnitza, Ariuşd, and Bulgarian Mound Culture complexes.

Since Childe (1948a, b) and Hawkes (1948) have recently summarized the evidence for cross-dating the Bronze and Iron Ages of Europe, it has seemed wise to close this paper with the end of the Aeneolithic period. Childe (1947, p. 122) has pointed out that most of the knot-headed pins and ingot torques of Cyprus and Syria fall between 2000 and 1700 B.C. and that the Unětice period thus probably begins about 1700 B.C.; Hawkes prefers a date a century earlier. It must be remembered, however, that knot-headed pins appear 1,000 years before this in Phases G and H in the Amouq (see Braidwood, p. 40, above), and they consequently cannot be considered as definitive criteria.

In this rapid survey it is evident that there are many gaps in the record which need to be filled and that some are more critical than others. First and foremost, a check excavation should be made at Vinča in order to unravel the stratigraphy. Good stratigraphic digging is needed in western Bulgaria to furnish reliable links between eastern Bulgaria, the middle Danube, and the south. In order to furnish soundly documented crossties between the Danube and Greece, both intensive and extensive work should be carried on in Macedonia.

With regard to the relative chronological linkages between the subareas of Continental Europe, the data still permit of considerable variation in interpretation. When it comes to anchoring the European sequences to those of the Aegean, Anatolia, and, through them, to Egypt and Mesopotamia, the evidence is sketchier still. In spite of the very great advances made during the last two decades, Nestor's remark (1933, p. 31) still contains much truth: "Jeder Forscher ein eigenes Lied singt."

PLATE I

Sources of illustrations; Provenience in parentheses.

Fig. 1.— Starčevo-Körös barbotine and plain ware. (a) Fewkes, Goldman, and Ehrich, Pl. VIII, 4 (Starčevo, Middle Danube); (b) Kutzian, Pl. XXI (eastern Hungary).

Fig. 2.— Black-on-red painted. (a, b) Fewkes, Goldman, and Ehrich, Pl. X, 24, 30 (Starčevo); (c) Wace and Thompson, Pl. I (Dimini, Thessaly); (d) Mylonas, Fig. 66a (Olynthus, Chalcidice).

Fig. 3.— Volute-Šarka-western Hungarian Linear-Bükk. (a) Jira, Pl. I (Podbaba, Praha, Bohemia); (b) Stocký, Pl. VIII, I (Praha, Bohemia); (c) Tompa, 1937, Pl. VIII, 1 (Békásmegyer, north-central Hungary); (d) Stocký, Pl. XXIX, 5 (Srbsko, Hořovice, west-central Bohemia); (e) Tompa, 1937, Pl. X, 4 (Aggtelek, northeastern Hungary).

Fig. 4.— Face lids. (a) Corpus Vasorum, Beograd 1, Pl. V, 9 (Vinča, middle Danube); (b) Blegen et al., Troy II, Pl. 79, 33.215 (Troy).

Fig. 5.— Dot-filled ribbons. (a) Vasić IV, Pl. XXXII, 75b (Vinča); (b) Corpus Vasorum, Belgrade 1, Pl. II, 9 (Vinča).

Fig. 6.— Cross-footed bowls. (a) Corpus Vasorum, Zagreb 1, Pl. VI, 2 (Vučedol, Slavonia); (b) Tompa, 1937, Pl. XX, 11 (Zók, southern Hungary).

Fig. 7.— Burnished and red-cross bowls. (a) Vasić II, Pl. XCVI, 362 (Vinča); (b) Blegen et al., Troy II, Pl. 246, 4a (Troy).

Fig. 8.— Socketed ladles. (a) Childe, 1929, Fig. 40a (Střelice, Moravia); (b) Rosetti, Fig. 27 (Vidra, Muntenia).

Fig. 9.— Peg-footed bowls. (a) Banner, Pl. XXXI, b (Kökénydomb, southeast Hungary); (b) Gaul, Pl. XXXVIII, 4 (Kodža Dermen, eastern Bulgaria).

Fig. 10.— Askoi. (a) Gaul, Pl. LV, 8 (Mečkur, south-central Bulgaria); (b) Nestor, Pl. VII, 4 (Salcutza, Oltenia); (c) Heurtley, No. 244 (Kilindír, Macedonia).

Fig. 11.— Tankards and cups. (a, b) Orssich de Slavetich, Fig. 13, 1, 2 (Bubanj, Niš district, Serbia); (c) Childe, 1929, Fig. 48 (Lengyel, western Hungary); (d) Tompa, 1937, Pl. XVIII, 13 (Tiszakeszi, Bodrogkeresztur culture, eastern Hungary); (e) Heurtley, No. 229 (Vardaróphtsa, Macedonia).

Fig. 12.— Tisza-type incision. (a) Mylonas, Fig. 59 (Olynthus, Chalcidice); (b) Tompa, 1929, Pl. XLIV, 5 (Öscsanád, eastern Hungary); (c) Childe, 1929, Fig. 43 (Lengyel, western Hungary).

Fig. 13.— Zoömorphic vessels with legs. (a) Mylonas, Fig. 35 (Olynthus, Chalcidice); (b) Böhm, Fig. 3 (Abraham, Slovakia).

Fig. 14.— Vădastra "B"-Phthiotic Thebes. (a) Gaul, Pl. LXV (Čakmak Tepe, northern Bulgaria); (b) Wace and Thompson, Fig. 113 (Phthiotic Thebes, east-central Greece).

PLATE I

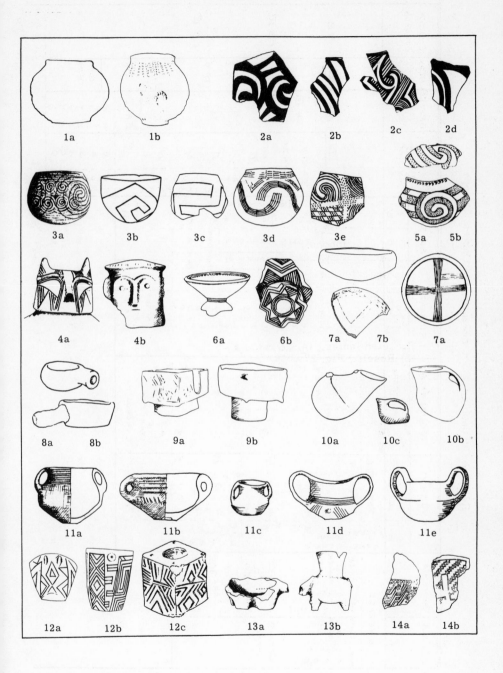

1a   1b   2a   2b   2c   2d

3a   3b   3c   3d   3e   5a   5b

4a   4b   6a   6b   7a   7b   7a

8a   8b   9a   9b   10a   10c   10b

11a   11b   11c   11d   11e

12a   12b   12c   13a   13b   14a   14b

Table 1

Relative Chronology of Southeastern and Central Europe

SILESIA	BOHEMIA	HUNGARY			JUGOSLAVIA			RUMANIA			BULGARIA		MACEDONIA THESSALY	GREECE	TROY	CILICIA (TARSUS)
		W	E	N	DRAVA MORAVA DANUBE (VINČA)			WALLACHIA TRANSYLVANIA MOLDAVIA			E	W				
UNĚTICE	UNĚTICE	TOSZEG B											MB IV	MH	VI	MB
MARSCHWITZ PREUNĚTICE	PREUNĚTICE	TOSZEG A				E II	VUČEDOL								V	
B C BELL BEAKER A R D E D N	B C BELL BEAKER A R D E D N	BELL BEAKER	BADEN		BADEN	E I		SCHNECKENBERG GUMELNIŞTA			III D		EARLY BRONZE	EH III	IV	EB III
				III									THESS. III		III	
JORDANS MÜHL	JORDANS MÜHL				D	S		C U C U T E N I A R I U Ş D			A G U M E L N I Ş T A C U C U T E N I		D	EH II	III δ	
STROKED (I b)	STROKED (I b)		II Ü II	K K	C	A II					P M A U R N I Ş A B E R L A E				II δ	EB II
ŠARKA	ŠARKA				V	R					S					
VOLUTE (I a)	VOLUTE (I a)		A I	K	B	A IB		TRANSITION			TRANSITION		D I N I	EH I	I	
		KÖRÖS STARČEVO			A? ŠIA			BOIAN A			BOIAN A		M O N I			
					STARČEVO KÖRÖS			KÖRÖS STARČEVO			STAR-ČEVO KÖRÖS		N I T H I C	NEO-DOLITHIC	KUM TEPE	

References

Banner, J. Die neolitische Ansiedlung von Kökénydomb, Dolgozatok, VI (1930), 107-58. Szeged.

Banner, J., and Parduz, M. Contributions nouvelles à l'histoire du Néolitique en Hongrie, pp. 30-41 ("Archaeologiai Értesítő Series III:" Vols. VII-VIII-IX.) Budapest, 1948.

Blegen, C. W.; Caskey, J. L.; Rawson, M.; and Sperling, J. Troy, Vol. I: General Introduction, the First and Second Settlements. Princeton: Princeton University Press, 1950.

Blegen, C. W.; Caskey, J. L.; and Rawson, M. Troy, Vol. II: The Third, Fourth, and Fifth Settlements. Princeton: Princeton University Press, 1951.

Böhm, J. "Zur Frage der Endphase der donauländischen Kultur," in Altböhmen und Altmähren, pp. 37-74. ("Mitteilungen für das Sudeten-Karpathenraumes.") Leipzig, 1942.

Buttler, W. Beiträge zur Frage des jungsteinzeitliche Handels, pp. 26-33. ("Marburger Studien," Vol. I.) Darmstadt, 1938.

_____. Der donauländische und der westische Kulturkreis der jüngeren Steinzeit. ("Handbuch der Urgeschichte Deutschlands," ed. E. Sprockhoff, Vol. 2.) Berlin and Leipzig: Walter de Gruyter & Co., 1938.

Childe, V. G. "Schipenitz: A Late Neolithic Station with Painted Pottery in Bukowina," Journal of the Royal Anthropological Institute of Great Britain and Ireland, LIII (1923), 263-88.

_____. The Danube in Prehistory. Oxford: Clarendon Press, 1929.

_____. 1937. Review of 25 Jahre Urgeschichtsforschung in Ungarn, 1912-36," by F. von Tompa, Proceedings of the Prehistoric Society, N. S., III (1937), 484-86.

_____. The Dawn of European Civilization. 4th ed. London: Kegan Paul, Trench & Trubner, 1947.

_____. "Cross Dating the European Bronze Age," Festschrift für Otto Tschumi, pp. 70-76. Frauenfeld: Huber, 1948.

_____. "The Final Bronze Age in the Near East and Temperate Europe," Proceedings of the Prehistoric Society, XIV (1948), 177-95.

_____. Prehistoric Migrations in Europe. Oslo, 1950.

_____. "Old World Prehistory: Neolithic." In: Kroeber, A., Anthropology Today, pp. 193-210. Chicago: University of Chicago Press, 1953.

Demangel, R. Le Tumulus dit de Protésilas. Paris: E. de Boccard, 1926.

Fewkes, V. J. "Excavations in the Late Neolithic Fortress of Homolka in Bohemia," Proceedings of the American Philosophical Society, LXXI (1932), 357-92.

_____. "Neolithic Sites in the Morava-Danubian Area (Eastern Yugoslavia)," Bulletin of the American School of Prehistoric Research, XII (1936), 5-82.

_____. "Neolithic Sites in the Yugoslavian Portion of the Lower Danubian Valley," Proceedings of the American Philosophical Society, LXXVIII (1937), 329-402.

Fewkes, V. J.; Goldman, H.; and Ehrich, R. W. "Excavations at Starčevo, Yugoslavia," Bulletin of the American School of Prehistoric Research, IX (1933); 33-51.

Gaul, J. H. "The Neolithic Period in Bulgaria," Bulletin of the American School of Prehistoric Research, Vol. XVI (1948).

Goldman, Hetty. Excavations at Eutrèsis in Boeotia. Cambridge: Harvard University Press, 1931.

Hawkes, C. F. C. The Prehistoric Foundations of Europe to the Mycenean Age. London: Methuen, 1940.

_____. "From Bronze Age to Iron Age: Middle Europe, Italy, the North, and West," Proceedings of the Prehistoric Society, XIV (1948), 196-218.

Heurtley, W. A. Prehistoric Macedonia. Cambridge: At the University Press, 1939.

Holste, F. "Zur chronologischen Stellung der Vinča-Keramik," Wiener prähistorische Zeitschrift, XXVI (1939), 1-21.

Jira, J. "Neolitische bemalte Keramik in Böhmen," Mannus, III (1911), 225-54.

Kastner, J. F. "Funde der Vučedol (Laibacher)-Kultur und der Glocken-becher Kultur von Aspern," Wiener prähistorische Zeitschrift, XXVI (1939), 117-34.

Korek, Jozsef. "A Settlement Belonging to the Bükk Culture in Oros (County Szabolcs)," Archaeologiai Értesítö, LXXVIII (1951), 72.

Kutzian, Ida. The Körös Culture. ("Dissertationes Pannonicae," Ser. II, No. 23.) Budapest, Plates 1944, Text 1947.

Milojčić, V. Chronologie der jüngeren Steinzeit Mittel- und Südosteuropas. Berlin: Mann, 1949.

_____. "Southeastern Elements in the Prehistoric Civilization of Serbia," Annual of the British School at Athens, XLIV (1949), 258-306.

Mozsolics, Amalia. Der Frühbronzezeitliche Urnenfriedhof von Kisapostag. ("Archaeologia Hungarica," Vol. XXVI.) Budapest, 1942.

_____. "Zur Frage der Schnurkeramik in Ungarn," Wiener prähisto-rische Zeitschrift, XXIX (1942), 30-50.

Mylonas, G. E. Excavations at Olynthus, Part I: The Neolithic Settle-ment. Baltimore: Johns Hopkins Press, 1929.

Nestor, J. Der Stand der Vorgeschichtsforschung in Rumänien, pp. 1-181. ("Bericht der Römisch-germanischen Kommission 1932," Vol. XXII.) Frankfurt on the Main, 1933.

Orssich de Slavetich, A. Bubanj, eine vorgeschichtliche Ansiedlung bei Niš. ("Mitteilungen der prähistorischen Kommission der Akademie der Wissenschaften, Vol. IV, Nos. 1-2.) Vienna, 1940.

Patay, P. Frühbronzezeitliche Kulturen in Ungarn. ("Dissertationes Pannonicae," Ser. II, No. 13.) Budapest, 1937.

Pittioni, R. Beiträge zur Urgeschichte der Landschaft Burgenland im Reichsgau Niederdonau. Wien: Franz Deuticke, 1941.

Rosetti, D. V. Sapaturile dela Vidra, raport preliminar. Bucharest: Publicatile Muzeului Municipiuli Bucurest, 1934.

Roska, M. "La Stratigraphie du Néolithique en Transylvanie," Dolgozatok, XII (1936), 42-51.

Schmidt, R. R. Die Burg Vučedol. Zagreb: Ausgabe des Kroatischen Archäologischen Staatsmuseums in Zagreb, 1945.

Schránil, J. Die Vorgeschichte Böhmens und Mährens. Berlin and Leipzig: Walter de Gruyter & Co., 1927, 1928.

Seger, H. "Jordansmühler Typus," Reallexikon der Vorgeschichte, ed. M. Ebert, VI (1926), 168-69.

_____. "Marschwitzer Typus," ibid., VIII (1927), 48-50.

Stocký, A. La Bohême préhistorique. I: L'Âge de Pierre. Prague: Musée National de Prague, 1929.

Tompa, F. Die Bandkeramik in Ungarn. ("Archaeologia Hungarica," Vols. V-VI.) Budapest, 1929.

_____. 25 Jahre Urgeschichtsforschung in Ungarn 1912-1936, pp. 27-127. ("Bericht der Römisch-germanischen Kommission 1934/1935," Nos. 24/25.) Berlin, 1937.

Vasić, M. M. Preistoriska Vinča II. Beograd, 1936.

_____. Preistoriska Vinča IV. Beograd, 1936.

Wace, A. J. B., and Thompson, M. S. Prehistoric Thessaly. Cambridge: At the University Press, 1912.

Weinberg, Saul S. "Aegean Chronology: Neolithic Period and Early Bronze Age," American Journal of Archaeology, LI (1947), 165-82.

_____. Review of Chronologie der jüngeren Steinzeit Mittel- und Südosteuropas by V. Milojčić, American Journal of Archaeology, LV (1951), 404-9.

Wilke, G. "Zselizer Typus," Reallexikon der Vorgeschichte, ed. M. Ebert, XIV (1929), 547.

Willvonseder, K. "Funde des Kreises Vučedol-Laibach aus Niederdonau und Ungarn," Wiener prähistorische Zeitschrift, XXVI (1939), 135-47.

The Relative Chronology of China through the Han Period

Lauriston Ward
Harvard University

No civilization ever developed in a vacuum. This is quite evident in the case of the early high cultures of Egypt, the Near East, and the Aegean, which arose in lands closely adjoining one another. It is less clear in the case of China, which lies on the other side of Asia. Yet, thanks to the archeological work of recent years, it is impossible to escape the conviction that China, in spite of its remote position, has always been in more or less intimate, though indirect, contact with the West and that many of the fundamental elements of Chinese culture had their origin in the countries near the Mediterranean Sea.

Notwithstanding this fact, few serious attempts have been made to relate the prehistoric and early historic phases of Chinese cultural development with those of the region which had its center in the eastern Mediterranean. This is partly because most experts who deal with Chinese archeology have not had an equal familiarity with the archeology of the rest of the Old World. A more fundamental reason, however, is the lack of excavation in the area intervening between the Near East and the Far East. From Anau, which lies on the northeastern edge of the Iranian cultural region, to central Kansu, which lies on the western edge of the Chinese cultural region, the distance is about 2,500 miles in an air line and longer by road. The area between, comprising most of Russian Turkestan and Chinese Turkestan, has until very recently been an absolute archeological blank for all periods preceding the last few centuries before the Christian Era. It is even now largely unknown. Any effort, therefore, to establish an exact chronological correlation between eastern and western Asia is beset with difficulties. Yet, in view of new material which has now come to light, it seems high time to attack this problem and at least to survey all the available evidence, even though the results cannot be expressed in the form of a comparative chronological chart.

The starting point for any attempt to date the early archeological remains of the Far East must be the critical use of the Chinese historical records. In so far as these can be considered trustworthy, they furnish a basis for exact correlation of Chinese remains with those of western Asia, which can also be dated by written records. Chinese historians report the existence of an early dynasty, the Hsia, which must still be considered more or less legendary. This was followed by the Shang dynasty, the reality of which has been partly confirmed by inscriptions on oracle bones found at the site of Anyang. The Shang dynasty was followed in turn by the Chou, Ch'in, and Han. The actual dates for these dynasties and their rulers are still somewhat in dispute, for there are three systems of chronology in use, namely, the "orthodox" system, based on the Han Shu, written in the first century A.D.; the system of the Bamboo Books, believed to have been compiled in the third century B.C., although the existing text is generally considered to be a forgery; and the system based on a revision of the Bamboo Books by Wang Kuo-wei, who put together quotations from the original text which appear in other works. From about the ninth century B.C., all three systems are in agreement and record the removal of the original Chou capital to the east in 771 B.C., the end of the Chou dynasty and the beginning of the Ch'in dynasty in 221 B.C., and the duration of the Han dynasty from 202 B.C. to A.D. 220. For the earlier period there is a marked divergence. The "orthodox" dates for the Shang dynasty are 1766-1122 B.C.; the Bamboo dates, 1558-1050 B.C.; and the revised Bamboo dates, 1523-1027 B.C. (Bishop, 1932; Creel, 1937). Most scholars believe that the two versions of the Bamboo dates are the more trustworthy and that they are not far from being historically correct. Even these, however, must be used with caution by the archeologist, for what we know of Shang culture archeologically is based on the remains excavated at the site of Anyang, in northern Honan, and Anyang was not founded, according to the records, until well on into the time of the Shang dynasty and was destroyed before the end of that dynasty. The recorded dates for Shang culture, then, as we know it archeologically, must be approximately from 1300 to 1100 B.C. This is a fact that many investigators have ignored. The Russians, in particular, tend to date Shang remains back to 1766 B.C.—a manifest error, which throws correlations with Siberian cultures far out of line.

Turning from history to archeology and the artifacts that have been recovered from excavated sites, we find that those in the North China plain have been grouped together into a series of early cultures, which are supposed to have succeeded one another in the following order: the Paleolithic culture of Chou-k'ou-tien; the late Paleolithic or early Meso-

lithic culture of the "Upper Cave" of Chou-k'ou-tien; the Red Pottery or
Painted Pottery or Yang-shao culture, and the Black Pottery or Lungshan
culture, both of which are apparently late Neolithic; the Bronze Age Shang
culture, which is at least semihistoric; and the fully historic Chou and
Han cultures (Wu, 1938; Bishop, 1939, 1942; Andersson, 1943; Loehr, 1952).
The first two of these are outside the scope of the present discussion, but
something must be said about the relative age of the two Neolithic cultures
before we turn to the problem of correlation with the West.

The relative dating of the Chinese Neolithic cultures is far from clear.
At one site at least, Hou Kang, in northern Honan, painted pottery of Yang-
shao type was found underlying characteristic black ware, which, in turn,
lay beneath Shang remains (Liang, 1933). Accordingly, it is customary to
say that the Red Pottery culture was earlier than the Black Pottery culture
and that both preceded the Shang culture. However, this is altogether too
simple a statement of a situation which appears to be highly complex. In
the first place, practically all the Red Pottery sites are located in the western part of the North China plain, and all the sites which are classed as belonging to the Black Pottery culture are in the eastern part of the plain;
hence the distinction between the two seems to be more geographical than
chronological. In the second place, while the classic Black Pottery sites
in eastern China contain no painted pottery, most of the Red Pottery sites
in western China contain some vessels and sherds of a ware which seems,
both in technique and in shape, to be similar to that found in the Black Pottery sites to the east. Furthermore, the stone and bone artifacts of both
cultures are almost identical, and we thus have two so-called "cultures"
that are classed as distinct solely on the basis of their most characteristic
pottery. This confusing set of facts might be explained by the hypothesis
that at one time there was a uniform Neolithic culture throughout the whole
North China plain, one feature of which was black pottery; and that at a
later date painted pottery was introduced into the western part of the area,
without altogether displacing the original black ware. Finally, much of
the conflicting evidence can perhaps be reconciled if we assume that the
Red Pottery and the Black Pottery cultures were to a large extent contemporary with each other and existed side by side for a considerable period
of time but that some of the Red Pottery sites, such as that of Yang-shao,
were earlier than some of the Black Pottery sites, such as Ch'êng-tzǔ-yai,
lower level, thus accounting for the stratigraphy at Hou Kang, which sig-
nificantly is situated on the border line between the areas of the two cul-

tures. There is also reason to believe that the Red Pottery and Black Pottery cultures did not come to an abrupt end with the advent of the Shang culture, which has thus far been found only in a small area in northern Honan, but that they continued in their respective regions long after the founding of Anyang.

We are not quite through with complications, however, for all the Neolithic sites of North China, Red Pottery and Black Pottery alike, contain another ceramic ware, characterized by mat-marking and cord-marking; this ware is closely related to pottery found widely extended in eastern Asia, from Siberia in the north to Indochina and Malaya in the south. Accompanying this pottery in North China are also polished stone celts, identical with those which are associated with the mat-marked and cord-marked pottery of Siberia, Indochina, and Malaya. If these relationships are valid, it must have taken a considerable time to produce such a wide diffusion of these traits through the eastern half of Asia, and one must assume that the first appearance of this type of pottery and the polished stone celts in the North China plain antedated the comparatively late development of the painted pottery and black ware in that area. The proof of this would lie in the discovery of sites containing mat-marked pottery and polished stone celts, without either painted pottery or black ware. So far, no such sites have been reported in North China, the presence of black ware in Pu Chao Chai in western Honan preventing it from being considered in this category. Yet it seems almost inevitable that such sites will ultimately be found—and this is all the more likely, since we know of no archeological remains to fill the great interval of time between the "Upper Cave" of Chou-k'ou-tien and the first appearance of the Red Pottery culture. Accordingly, it seems best, on the basis of existing evidence, to break down the Neolithic of the North China plain into three cultures: a hypothetical Early Neolithic culture, which was followed in time by two late Neolithic cultures, Red Pottery and Black Pottery, which were largely contemporary, though in certain cases the Red Pottery culture may be considered to be the earlier of the two.

If this interpretation is accepted, we are now ready to consider the evidence which relates the archeological remains of China with parallel occurrences in western Asia. As will soon be seen, this evidence is very extensive and leaves no doubt that there were many connections between China and the West at different periods of time. But, unfortunately, the parallels are usually general in their nature and do not yet permit close and accurate dating in terms of the prehistoric and early historic culture sequences in the Near East and Europe. Accordingly, the rest of this paper will be in the nature of a survey of the pertinent evidence, which will serve more as a guide to further investigation than as a statement of final conclusions. In spite of these limitations, the subject is so important that even a tentative approach to the problem may have its value, all the more so as few attempts have ever been made to assemble all the evidence and only one of them, the excellent critical article by Max Loehr (1952), is recent enough to make use of the latest material.

The polished stone celts of the hypothetical Early Neolithic culture of China, which is as yet represented only by survivals in sites of later cultures, are similar to those found throughout Asia, from the Near East to the Malay Peninsula. They are useless for precise dating. The earliest-known occurrences in the Near East are at Hassuna (Lloyd et al., 1945) and Jarmo (Braidwood, 1951), to which a date in the fifth millennium B.C. may be assigned. The mat-marked and cord-marked ware has a wide but more limited distribution, occurring with celts in the earliest Neolithic sites of Siberia (Okladnikov, 1950) and elsewhere in eastern and southeastern Asia. No sure date can be given for the Siberian remains. Tentatively, we may assign them to some time between 3000 and 2000 B.C. In western Asia early mat-marked pottery is, to the best of the author's knowledge, entirely absent, with the exception of one puzzling occurrence at the site of Tabbat-al-Hammam on the Syrian coast, where it seems to be associated with sherds of Halaf type and may perhaps be even earlier than the Halaf period (Braidwood, 1940). In India, also, there is a striking case of cord-marked sherds found at the "megalithic" site of Bursahom, in Kashmir. The date of Bursahom is uncertain, although De Terra (1942) considers it to be very early. On the basis of the polished celts, one is forced to the unsatisfactory conclusion that the hypothetical Early Neolithic culture of China, if it really existed, may have been as early as 5000 B.C.; but if the diffusion was from west to east, it could be much later, perhaps a thousand or two years later.

The late Neolithic sites of the Red Pottery or Yang-shao culture in the western part of the North China plain show the use of agriculture, notably the cultivation of millet, which may have been introduced from the West, and possibly rice, which would presumably have come from southern Asia. The striking feature of these sites, however, is the painted pottery, which is clearly in the general ceramic tradition of the Near Eastern countries and which is not found elsewhere in eastern Asia, with the exception of a slight extension into southern Manchuria (Andersson, 1923a, b, 1947; Arne, 1925; Liang, 1930). The predominant type of the pottery is black-on-red, which is the prevailing style in the northern part of the Iranian area, at the other end of the route leading from Russian Turkestan to China. Individual decorative motifs have their parallels in the prehistoric pottery of northern Iran, but the relationship is not close enough to tie them up to any one site in that area. On the whole, the geometric designs of the Chinese pottery, such as lattice-work and triangles with slightly curving sides, suggest more nearly the wares of Anau I than those of any other fully known site in the West but do not afford grounds for belief that the Chinese pottery was directly influenced by Anau but rather that it was descended from a common ancestor, which preceded Anau I (Pumpelly, 1908). Opinions vary as to the date of the Anau I culture. For reasons which cannot be detailed here, the best estimate would seem to be that it flourished from about 4000 to 3000 B.C. A few simple copper objects are found in the Anau I levels, while none have yet been reported in the Red Pottery sites, which tends to indicate that the Chinese culture was descended from, or influenced by, an early Neolithic culture in the northern Iranian area and that copper metallurgy, which was beginning to be practiced by the first inhabitants of Anau, did not spread to China until a much later date. There are some slight similarities between the Anau I stone and bone artifacts and those of the Chinese sites, though not enough to be seriously stressed, as the industries in general are quite dissimilar. Somewhat more suggestive, though not altogether convincing, are the solid-footed tripod vessels of Yang-shao (Andersson, 1947, pp. 32-33 and Pl. 2) and others from Giyan III and Djamshidi III in Iran (Contenau and Ghirshman, 1935, Pls. 25-29 and 74-78) and Troy II in Anatolia (Blegen, 1950, Pl. 406). The dates of the two Iranian levels are estimated to be somewhere between 2500 and 1800 B.C., and Troy II falls within the same time range. Reference should also be made, for what it is worth, to the use of a white slip on some of the Red Pottery painted sherds from Hsi-yin-tsun in southwestern Shansi and the presence of a white-slipped ware in Giyan III (Liang, 1930, p. 22; Contenau and Ghirshman, 1935, p. 70).

The possibility and, indeed, the probability that the Chinese and Iranian painted wares are truly related, in spite of the 3000 miles that lie between them, is greatly strengthened by the fact that pottery, of uncertain date but in the same general painted ceramic tradition, has been found in

the province of Kansu (see below) and near Hami and Turfan in Chinese
Turkestan (Bergman, 1939, pp. 14-26), while the Russians report pottery
of Anau type at a number of unpublished sites to the northeast of Anau,
along the slopes of the Tian Shan mountains (Avdiev, 1942, p. 67). This
reduces the gap to a matter of some 1000 miles, in an area through which
ran the main route connecting western with eastern Asia.

The painted pottery found by Andersson at many sites in Kansu must
be more carefully considered in this connection (Andersson, 1925, 1945;
Palmgren, 1934; Pelzel, 1940; Bylin-Althin, 1946; Nae, 1946; Loehr, 1948).
As is well known, Andersson classified these sites into six chronological
stages, beginning with Ch'i Chia and continuing through Pan Shan, Ma
Chang, Hsin Tien, Ssu Wa, and Sha Ching. The only stratigraphic basis
for such a relative dating is in the case of Hsin Tien, which is definitely
later than Pan Shan, because at one site sherds of Hsin Tien overlay those
of Pan Shan. The Ch'i Chia sites are now generally considered to be more
or less contemporary with Pan Shan, leaving the other three stages rather
floating in time, although the presence of copper in some of them would
tend to mark them as later than Ch'i Chia and Pan Shan, in which metal
is absent.

Now there is one possible tie-up with the West, in the case of the typical Pan Shan ware, which, both in shape and in design, has close parallels
in the Tripolye B culture of the Ukraine (Passek, 1935) and in Cucuteni B
in the Balkans (Schmidt, 1932). Indeed, the similarities are so marked
that one is strongly inclined to credit the relationship and thus assign a
date of about 2200-1700 B.C. for the Pan Shan culture. This does not help
us much, however, in dating archeological remains on the North China
plain, for the Pan Shan pottery is, on the whole, quite different from that
of Yang-shao, and, while there is a tendency to relate the two by way of
parallels to both in some of the sites in southern Kansu, such a procedure
does not give us complete assurance that they were of the same age. Let
us say, then, that the Red Pottery culture on this basis may be contemporary with the Pan Shan stage of Kansu and thus perhaps was flourishing
during the period just before and just after 2000 B.C.—a conclusion which
does not do violence to the rest of the archeological evidence in China.

The Black Pottery sites of North China (Fu et al., 1934; Plumer, 1935;
Drake, 1940; Liang, 1940; Beath, 1941; Kaplan, 1948-49; Chêng, 1949) show
several new parallels with the West, notably in the presence of bones of
presumably domesticated sheep and oxen. The sheep are of the western

or Urial type, and there are no indigenous cattle in China; so both were probably introduced from central or western Asia. The use of the potter's wheel is also now reported for the first time in China. None of these traits give good ground for any precise dating of the Black Pottery culture. Cattle and sheep were domesticated in the Near East as early as the fifth millennium B.C. Wheel-made pottery occurs in the Iranian area as early as Hissar Ib in Iran (Schmidt, 1937) and Anau III in Russian Turkestan (Pumpelly, 1908). Preferred dates for the latter are about 2500-2000 B.C. or even later. If the potter's wheel diffused from west to east, as seems likely, this would make the Black Pottery culture later than 2500 B.C., perhaps considerably later, to allow for time lag.

The most useful trait for comparative purposes, however, is the black pottery itself. This is characteristically light-gray to dark-gray or black in color, with a surface that is often highly burnished. This ware invites comparisons with that which replaces painted wares in Anau II and Hissar II and also with the gray-burnished ware of Troy V-VII (Blegen et al., 1951, Part I, p. 235), which, in turn, has been likened to the Minyan ware of Greece. The similarity, indeed, goes a step further than surface and color. The type shape in Hissar II and to some extent in Anau II as well (Schmidt, 1937, p. 112 and Figs. 68, 70; Pumpelly, 1908, I, 134) is a hollow pedestaled cup with concave flaring base and rim. The same shape is found in the black pottery of China, and it was extremely common in the lower level of Ch'êng-tzŭ-yai (Fu et al., 1934, p. 18 and Pl. XVIII, Figs. 1-3). Furthermore, the pedestal was often decorated by two or three fine raised rings. A specimen of this type from Hissar II, which is now in the Peabody Museum at Harvard, is almost identical with one illustrated in the Ch'êng-tzŭ-yai report (ibid., Pl. XXIII, No. 9).

Accompanying this typical black ware, which, in spite of its name, is often gray in color, is a true black ware, with extremely thin walls and a highly polished surface. Similar very thin, black polished pottery occurs sparingly in the upper part of the main level of Chashmah Ali (Rayy) in northern Iran (sherds in Peabody Museum, Harvard University), where it is associated with other pottery which shows it to be contemporary with Hissar Ic. This thin black ware also occurs in the Chalcolithic level of Alishar Hüyük in Anatolia (Von der Osten, 1937, p. 54 and Fig. 67) and rarely in Early Dynastic I levels of southern Mesopotamia. Most of the western parallels, with the exception of the Minyan ware of Troy and Greece, fall within the period from 3000 to 2400 B.C. This is too early for the end of the classic period of the Black Pottery culture, which, near Anyang at least, immediately preceded the Shang culture; but we have no certain way of dating the beginning of the Black Pottery culture in China, which in western Honan perhaps coincided with the beginning of the Red Pottery culture. Also an ample allowance of time must be made for the diffusion of the black pottery from Iran and Russian Turkestan to the North China plain.

When we come to discuss the Shang culture, we are on somewhat surer chronological ground (Li Chi, 1929-33; Academia Sinica, 1933-35; Pelliot, 1937; Lin, 1938). Here we meet with a further series of cultural traits which almost certainly had their origin in western Asia. Among these are wheat, domesticated horses not of native Mongolian type, and chariots drawn by two horses yoked abreast. To these may perhaps be added bronze metallurgy and writing, both of which were known in the West at a time much earlier than any date that can possibly be assigned to the Shang remains at Anyang. One of the traits just mentioned, namely, wheat, goes back to the fifth millennium B.C. More helpful evidence for actual dating purposes may be found in the bronze artifacts. Some of these, such as the bronze ceremonial vessels, are like nothing in the West, as are also certain types of weapons. There are, however, other bronze artifacts from Anyang which are of convincingly Western type, namely, helmets (cf. Early Dynastic forms in Mesopotamia), socketed celts of European Late Bronze Age type, and socketed spearheads with two loops for binding, like those occurring in Europe in the Middle Bronze Age (Seligman, 1920; Childe, 1930, pp. 66-67 and 92-93; Karlgren, 1945). If an archeological complex must always be dated by the latest of its components, then the Shang culture of North China cannot be considered to be much earlier than the beginning of the Late Bronze Age of Europe. This agrees quite well with the historical dates for Anyang, i.e., about 1300-1100 B.C., without precluding a slightly later date, if one feels that the historical dates are not entirely accurate.

With the culture of the Chou period, we begin to emerge into the full light of history. At the same time, there are relatively few archeological features which can serve to tie up China chronologically with the West. Swords of bronze and iron, of presumably Chou date, are like Western specimens, and some, indeed, closely resemble the Hallstatt sword with antennae, but they do not come from excavated sites, so their exact chronological position is uncertain (Janse, 1930a, b). From historical records we learn that iron was used to some extent in North China by the middle of the seventh century B.C. Glazed pottery perhaps began to be made in Late Chou times, as is shown by specimens from tombs thought to be of that age in Chang-sha, south of the Yangtze River (personal communication from John H. Cox). This first use of glaze in China may or may not be due to Western influence.

It was in Han times that commerce between China and the Roman world became fully established, along the ancient Central Asiatic trade route and also by sea. Chinese silk was exported to the West, and certain articles of luxury were received in exchange. This we know from historical records rather than from archeological sources, for hardly any Han habitation sites in China proper have been excavated or even investigated. Some undocumented material of this period has been reported, notably glass beads of Syrian and Egyptian manufacture, the earliest of which, according to Seligman, may even antedate the Han dynasty by a few years (Seligman, 1937; Seligman and Beck, 1938).

This concludes our survey of the evidence which may be used to correlate the prehistoric and early historic archeology of China with that of western Asia. There is, it is true, another line of approach to this problem, namely, the attempt to date Chinese objects in terms of the sequence of cultures in southern Siberia, particularly in the Minusinsk region. It is impossible here to deal adequately with this very complicated question, important as it is for students of the Asiatic past. On the one hand, the documentation of Chinese objects which have been compared with those of Siberia is not always good. On the other hand, the documentation of the Siberian parallels is not always certain either. Some bronze artifacts, for example, have been assigned to one or another of the Minusinsk cultures on the basis of illustrations in Teploukhov's famous report, although their attribution to these cultures is not borne out by the text of the report. Finally, even if the Sino-Siberian comparisons were all sound and exact, it is difficult to correlate the Siberian Neolithic and Bronze Age cultures with those of the Near East and European Russia, and archeologists are still far from agreement on Siberian dates for any period before the Kara Suk, beginning about 1200 or 1100 B.C. So this phase of our problem will have to be passed over, with a mention only (Teploukhov, 1927, 1929; Gaul, 1943; Loehr, 1949; Jettmar, 1950; Kiselev, 1951).

Reviewing, now, all the evidence which has been so summarily discussed, it is perhaps possible to arrive at a few general conclusions.

1. It seems quite clear that China was never separated from the rest of Asia by an iron curtain and that the development of Chinese culture was stimulated from period to period by the acceptance of traits, many of them fundamental, which had their origin in western Asia.

2. In most cases probably these traits were not diffused directly from Iran, let us say, to the North China plain but passed gradually through central Asia, from people to people and with many modifications en route, until they ultimately reached China.

3. For this reason it is extremely difficult to assign accurate dates to the early Chinese cultures on the basis of Western traits which they contain, for it is impossible to know in each case how long it took for the diffusion from west to east. Often, apparently, this was a matter of centuries and sometimes perhaps even tens of centuries.

4. So, until there is adequate excavation of early sites in the area intervening between west and east, i.e., in Russian Turkestan, Zungaria, and Chinese Turkestan, no more definite correlation can be seriously attempted, and any comparative chronological table that might be drawn up would only show the dates at which the traits borrowed by the Chinese first appeared in the Near East and not the dates at which they arrived in China. Such a table would be so highly speculative and misleading that it will not be attempted here.

5. In spite of these difficulties, a survey of all the evidence connecting Chinese cultures with those of the West, even such a brief one as the present effort, may be useful, particularly as some of this evidence is here presented for the first time. Furthermore, this survey will at least call attention to the urgency of the problem and perhaps stimulate further research on the part of students of Chinese archeology, who are usually not too familiar with the details of the archeology of western Asia, and on the part of Near Eastern experts, who are generally quite unfamiliar with the Far East and its archeological problems. Only by co-operation between these two groups of scholars can we hope for a satisfactory solution.

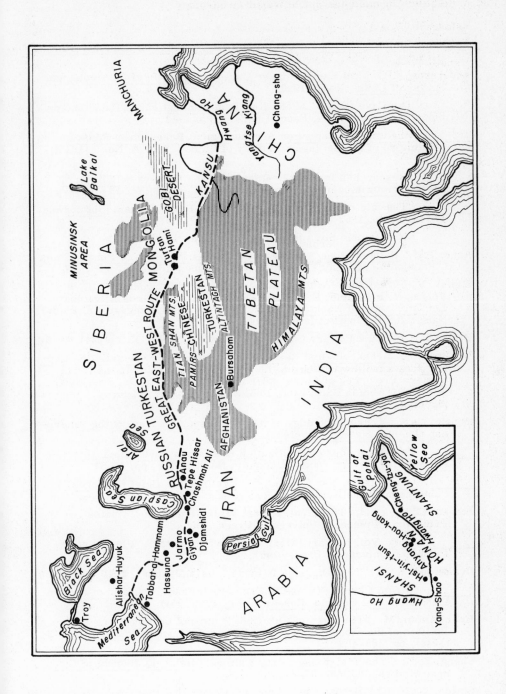

References

Academia Sinica. Studies Presented to Tsai Yuan Pei on His Sixty-fifth Birthday. 2 vols. 1933-35. (In Chinese.)

Andersson, J. G. "An Early Chinese Culture," Bulletin of the Geological Survey of China, No. 5 (1923).

──────. The Cave Deposit at Sha Kuo T'un in Fengtien. ("Palaeontologia Sinica," Ser. D, Vol. I, Fasc. 1 [1923]), pp. 1-43.

──────. Preliminary Report on Archaeological Research in Kansu. ("Memoirs of the Geological Survey of China," Ser. A, No. 5 [1925]), pp. 1-51.

──────. "Researches into the Prehistory of the Chinese," Bulletin of the Stockholm Museum of Far Eastern Antiquities, No. 15 (1943).

──────. "The Site of Chu Chia Chai, Hsi Ning Hsien, Kansu," ibid., No. 17 (1945), pp. 1-63.

──────. "Prehistoric Sites in Honan," ibid., No. 19 (1947).

Arne, T. J. Painted Stone Age Pottery from the Province of Honan, China ("Palaeontologia Sinica," Ser. D, Vol. I, Fasc. 2 [1925]), pp. 1-40.

Avdiev, V. I. "Istoriko-Arkheologicheskoe Izuchenie Srednei Azii. In: Volgin, V. P.; Tarle, E. V.; and Pankratova, A. M. (eds.) Dvadtsat' Let Istoricheskoi Nauki v S.S.S.R. Moscow and Leningrad: Akademiia Nauk S.S.S.R., Institut Istorii, 1942.

Beath, S. S. "Black Pottery Culture in Chekiang," Asia, XLI (1941), 47-51.

Bergman, F. Archaeological Researches in Sinkiang, Especially the Lop-Nor Region. ("Reports from the Scientific Expedition to the North-western Provinces of China under the Leadership of Dr. Sven Hedin, The Sino-Swedish Expedition, Pub. No. 7, VII: "Archaeology," 1 [1939]).

Bishop, C. W. "The Chronology of Ancient China," Journal of the American Oriental Society, LII (1932), 232-47.

──────. The Beginnings of Civilization in Eastern Asia, Suppl. to Journal of the American Oriental Society, No. 4 (1939), pp. 45-61.

──────. Origin of the Far Eastern Civilizations: A Brief Handbook. ("Smithsonian Institution War Background Studies," No. 1 [1942]).

Blegen, C. W., et al. Troy, Vol. I, Part I (text) and Part II (plates). Princeton: Princeton University Press, 1950.

──────. Troy, Vol. II, Part I (test) and Part II (plates). Princeton: Princeton University Press, 1951.

Braidwood, R. J. "Test Diggings in Syria," Asia, January, 1940, pp. 47-50.

──────. "From Cave to Village in Prehistoric Iraq," Bulletin of the American Schools of Oriental Research, No. 124 (1951), pp. 12-18.

Bylin-Althin, M. "The Sites of Ch'i Chia P'ing and Lo Han T'ang in Kansu," Bulletin of the Stockholm Museum of Far Eastern Antiquities, No. 18 (1946), pp. 383-498.

Chêng, T. K. "The T'ai-p'ing-ch'ang Culture," Hsieh-ta Journal of Chinese Studies, I (1949), 67-81.

Childe, V. G., The Bronze Age. London: Cambridge University Press, 1930.

Contenau, G., and Ghirshman, R. Fouilles du Tépé-Giyan, près de Néhavend, 1931 et 1932. Paris: Librairie Orientaliste Paul Geuthner, 1935.

Creel, H. G. Studies in Early Chinese Culture, First Series. ("American Council of Learned Societies, Studies in Chinese and Related Civilizations," No. 3.) Baltimore: Waverly Press, 1937.

de Terra, H. "The Megaliths of Bursahom, Kashmir: A New Prehistoric Civilization from India," American Philosophical Society Proceedings, LXXXV (1942), 483-504.

Drake, F. S. "Ancient Chinese Pottery from Shantung," Monumenta Serica, IV, Fasc. 2 (1940), 383-405.

Fu, S. N., et al. "Ch'êng-tzŭ-yai: A Report of Excavations of the Protohistoric Site at Ch'êng-tzŭ-yai, Li-ch'êng Hsien, Shantung. ("Archaeologia Sinica," No. 1[1934].)

Gaul, J. H. "Observations on the Bronze Age in the Yenisei Valley, Siberia," Peabody Museum Papers, Harvard University, XX (1943), 149-86.

Janse, O. "Notes sur quelques épées anciennes trouvées en Chine," Bulletin of the Stockholm Museum of Far Eastern Antiquities, No. 2 (1930), pp. 67-176.

_____. "Quelques antiquités chinoises d'un caractère hallstattien," ibid. (1930), pp. 177-92.

Jettmar, K. "The Karasuk Culture and Its Southeastern Affinities," Bulletin of the Stockholm Museum of Far Eastern Antiquities, No. 22 (1950), pp. 83-126.

Kaplan, S. M. "Early Pottery from the Liang Chu Site, Chekiang Province," Archives of the Chinese Art Society of America, III (1948-49), 13-42.

Karlgren, B. "Some Weapons and Tools of the Yin Dynasty," Bulletin of the Stockholm Museum of Far Eastern Antiquities, No. 17 (1945), pp. 101-44.

Kiselev, S. V. Drevniaia Istoriia iuzhnoĭ Sibiri. 2d ed. Moscow: Akademiia Nauk S.S.S.R., Institut Istorii Material'noĭ Kul'tury, 1951.

Liang, S. Y. New Stone Age Pottery from the Prehistoric Site at Hsi-yin Tsun, Shansi, China. ("Memoirs of the American Anthropological Association," No. 37 [1930].)

_____. "The Excavations at Hou-kang." In: Li Chi (ed.), Preliminary Reports of Excavations at An Yang, IV (1933), 609-26. (In Chinese.)

_____. "The Lungshan Culture," Quarterly Bulletin of Chinese Bibliography, N.S. I (1940), 251-62.

Li Chi (ed.). Preliminary Reports of Excavations at Anyang. 4 vols. 1929-33. (In Chinese.)

Lin, Y. H. "A Report on the Archaeological Site of Anyang, Honan, China: A Report for Anthropology 28 (Harvard University)." Unpublished MS, 1938.

Lloyd, S.; Safar, F.; and Braidwood, R. J. "Tell Hassuna, Excavations by the Iraq Government Directorate General of Antiquities in 1943 and 1944," Journal of Near Eastern Studies, IV, No. 4 (1945), 255-89.

Loehr, M. "China: Prehistoric Kansu," American Journal of Archaeology, LII, No. 2 (1948), 404-6.

_____. "Weapons and Tools from Anyang and Siberian Analogies," ibid., LIII, No. 2 (1949), 126-44.

_____. "Zur Ur- und Vorgeschichte Chinas," Saeculum, III (1952), 15-55.

Nae, S. "New Discovery of a Ch'i Chia Culture Cemetery," Journal of the Royal Anthropological Institute of Great Britain and Ireland, LXXVI, Part 2 (1946), 169-75.

Okladnikov, A. P. "Neolit i Bronzovyĭ Vek Pribaikal'ia," Materialy i Issledovaniia po Arkheologii S.S.R.R., No. 18. Moscow-Leningrad: Akademiia Nauk S.S.S.R., Institut Istorii Material'noĭ Kul'tury, 1950.

Osten, H. H. von der. The Alishar Hüyük, Seasons of 1930-32, Part I. Chicago: University of Chicago Press, 1937.

Palmgren, N. Kansu Mortuary Urns of the Pan Shan and Ma Chang Groups. ("Palaeontologia Sinica," Ser. D, Vol. III, Fasc. 1 [1934].)

Passek, T. La Céramique tripolienne. Moscow and Leningrad: Académie de l'histoire de la culture materielle, 1935.

Pelliot, P. "Royal Tombs of Anyang." In: Studies in Chinese Art and Some Indian Influences. London: The India Society, 1938.

Pelzel, J. "J. G. Andersson's Kansu Sites: A Report for Anthropology 28 (Harvard University)." Unpublished MS, 1940.

Plumer, J. M. "Early Pottery Fragments from Hangchow Bay," Journal of the Royal Asiatic Society, North China Branch, LXVI (1935), 115-16.

Pumpelly, R. Explorations in Turkestan. Expedition of 1904. ("Publications of the Carnegie Institution of Washington," No. 73.) 2 vols. 1908.

Schmidt, E. F. Excavations at Tepe Hissar, Damghan. Philadelphia: University of Pennsylvania Press, 1937.

Schmidt, H. Cucuteni in der Oberen Moldau. Berlin: Greuter, 1932.

Seligman, C. G. "Bird Chariots and Socketed Celts in Europe and China," Journal of the Royal Anthropological Institute of Great Britain and Ireland, L (1920), 153-58.

_____. "The Roman Orient and the Far East," Antiquity, XI (1937), 5-30.

Seligman, C. G., and Beck, H. C. "Far Eastern Glass: Some Western Origins," Bulletin of the Stockholm Museum of Far Eastern Antiquities, No. 10 (1938), pp. 1-64.

Teploukhov, S. A. "Drevnie Pogrebeniia v Minusinskom Krae," Materialy po Etnografii, III, Part 2 (1927), 57-112.

_____. "Opyt Klassifikatsii Drevnikh Metallicheskikh Kul'tur Minusinskogo Kraia," ibid., IV, Part 2 (1929), 41-62.

Wu, G. D. Prehistoric Pottery in China. London: Kegan Paul, Trench, Trubner & Co., 1938.

[The underscoring of page references indicates an entire article or a clearly titled section of which the subject is the theme. Numbered and lettered periods, phases, site levels, etc., are also underlined for clarity and ease in reading.]